W0114428

Praise for
What Your Comfort Costs Us

"Gabriela opened her heart to deliver a deeply personal and reflective journey through the experiences and challenges of women of color in leadership. This book can be particularly instructive to cis-men leaders wanting to foster empathy, deep inclusion, and mutuality in their organizations. By learning about Gabriela and other women leaders' experiences, men can help dismantle harmful structures that perpetuate inequality and restrict true freedom for all.

"Once you see the injustices women of color are experiencing, you can't unsee them."

—EFRAÍN GUTIÉRREZ, co-founder, Freedom Dreams in Philanthropy

"*What Your Comfort Costs Us* is part of an emerging and damning narrative about the experiences of women of color in leadership. Though race/ethnicity and gender are key shapers of how much power society thinks women of color should be able to wield, this is a woefully understudied area in leadership.

"The last few years saw an opening into leadership as organizations struggling with inequality tapped women of color to lead during extremely tumultuous times, with little support and heightened expectations. Now, a few years later, these leaders have horror stories to tell about their experiences, and they are breaking the rules in telling them. They also tell us what they need to be supported."

—CYNDI SUAREZ, author of *The Power Manual: How to Master Complex Power Dynamics*, former president and editor-in-chief of *Nonprofit Quarterly*

"*What Your Comfort Costs Us* is part personal story, part collective witnessing, and a challenge to workplaces—particularly those in the third sector—to step up. Dr. Alcalde adds an important critique to the growing literature on white supremacy in the workplace. Yet this book is for all of us who work, regardless of our racial background or gender expression, regardless of whether we have harmed others or been harmed. Most compelling is Dr. Alcalde's interrogation of workplace infrastructure itself and the invitation to dream up new models for getting things done. Can we imagine self-managed workplaces without hierarchy? Can we imagine workplaces rooted in Indigenous wisdom alive in social philosophies like buen vivir?

"Dr. Alcalde invites us to take a hard look at the workplaces we have inherited and experiment our way into a future where work looks nothing like it does today."

—YANIQUE REDWOOD, PhD, author of *White Women Cry and Call Me Angry*

"The powerful stories woven throughout this book provide a visceral illustration, at times gut-wrenching, of the struggles faced by and harm enacted on women of color in leadership positions. As an executive coach to women of color leaders, the stories are all too familiar. I love that this book rightly shifts the responsibility back to organizations to change the white-dominant workplace culture enacting the harm, instead of placing the burden on women to be more resilient.

"Not only does this book challenge us to critically examine traditional organizational structures and workplace culture, but it invites us to reimagine them, and to entertain new concepts of power and leadership that are not tied to capitalism, white supremacy, and patriarchy."

—ESTRELLA DAWSON, personal and executive coach, emotional intelligence trainer

WHAT YOUR COMFORT COSTS US

Women of Color Reimagining Leadership
and Transforming Workplace Culture to
Promote Dignity, Equity, and Liberation for All

M. GABRIELA ALCALDE, MPH, DrPH

North Atlantic Books
Huichin, unceded Ohlone land
Berkeley, California

Copyright © 2025 by M. Gabriela Alcalde. All rights reserved. No portion of this book, except for brief review, may be reproduced, stored in a retrieval system, or transmitted in any form or by any means—electronic, mechanical, photocopying, recording, or otherwise—without the written permission of the publisher. For information contact North Atlantic Books.

Published by
North Atlantic Books
Huichin, unceded Ohlone land
Berkeley, California

Cover art and design by Amanda Weiss
Book design by Happenstance Type-O-Rama

Printed in Canada

What Your Comfort Costs Us: Women of Color Reimagining Leadership and Transforming Workplace Culture to Promote Dignity, Equity, and Liberation for All is sponsored and published by North Atlantic Books, an educational nonprofit based in the unceded Ohlone land Huichin (Berkeley, CA) that collaborates with partners to develop cross-cultural perspectives; nurture holistic views of art, science, the humanities, and healing; and seed personal and global transformation by publishing work on the relationship of body, spirit, and nature.

North Atlantic Books's publications are distributed to the US trade and internationally by Penguin Random House Publisher Services. For further information, visit our website at www.northatlanticbooks.com.

Library of Congress Cataloging-in-Publication Data
Names: Alcalde, M. Gabriela, author.
Title: The cost of your comfort : strategies for equity, dignity, and liberation in the workplace / M. Gabriela Alcalde, MPH, DrPH.
Description: Berkeley, California : North Atlantic Books, [2025] | Includes bibliographical references and index. | Summary: "Drawing on the intersecting experiences of Black/African American, Latine, Asian, LGBTQ+, multi-racial, and immigrant women in nonprofit, philanthropic, and higher education sectors, this book addresses the need for structural and systemic change of workplace cultures"-- Provided by publisher.
Identifiers: LCCN 2024021034 (print) | LCCN 2024021035 (ebook) | ISBN 9798889842132 (paperback) | ISBN 9798889842149 (epub)
Subjects: LCSH: Racism in the workplace. | Discrimination in employment. | Sex discrimination in employment. | Diversity in the workplace.
Classification: LCC HF5549.5.R23 A43 2025 (print) | LCC HF5549.5.R23 (ebook) | DDC 658.30089--dc23/eng/20240607
LC record available at https://lccn.loc.gov/2024021034
LC ebook record available at https://lccn.loc.gov/2024021035.

1 2 3 4 5 6 7 8 9 FRIESENS 29 28 27 26 25

This book includes recycled material and material from well-managed forests. North Atlantic Books is committed to the protection of our environment. We print on recycled paper whenever possible and partner with printers who strive to use environmentally responsible practices.

To my pack.

Pilar, Xavier, Gonzalo, Cristina, Nico, Lucas, Rob

It is from the deep, strong roots of our shared love
that I can unfurl into my truest self.

What we don't see, we assume can't be.
What a destructive assumption.

—OCTAVIA E. BUTLER

Contents

SECTION 1
Claiming Space by Telling Our Stories

SECTION 2
Supremacist Origin Stories

SECTION 3
Silence and Inaction as Harm

SECTION 4
The System Will Not Be Complicit in Its Own Demise

SECTION 5
Leading Outside the Lines

Foreword

Transformative change will necessitate cultural metamorphosis across all dimensions of our worlds. While this book is focused on the changes that organizations and their cultures must undertake, it is impossible to talk about changing organizations and their cultures without talking about changing ourselves and healing our wounds.

—GABRIELA ALCALDE

In this book, Gabriela Alcalde celebrates the collective journeys of women whose identities span the global cultural diaspora, and she completes a nuanced perspective about the state of workplace dynamics within contemporary American institutions. With a mixture of rigor, care, and self-reflection, Gabriela showcases the real-life experiences of women of color serving in leadership roles, including herself, who have navigated nonprofit, philanthropic, and higher education workplaces in recent years. She outlines recurring challenges within organizational hierarchies, using firsthand accounts from women of color—providing a rare platform for a cohort whose voices have only recently been elevated within the mainstream discourse to tell their own stories. Gabriela offers a litany of references and proposes lessons for our collective organizational-transformation journeys to inform how we cultivate humanizing workplace conditions that affirm every person's value and reinforce connection for people representing diverse backgrounds.

This resonates with me on several levels.

As a longtime organizer and social justice practitioner . . . I have witnessed how the fervor and deep-seated conviction for societal change held by myself and generations of activists was undermined by the self-defeating impacts of unaddressed personal harm experienced over a lifetime of navigating inequitable relationships and systems. Only after years of self-exploration and ontological coaching was I able to equip myself with therapeutic practices that restore personal agency, sharpen discernment, clarify vision, and enable reconciliation with people across differing categories of identity. Before that, I had not learned how to operate with healthy emotional boundaries, which inhibited my ability to interact authentically and empathetically—*dynamically*—with people whose implicit biases subtly yet routinely exposed me to being dismissed, judged, assessed as safe, and made to feel as if my perspective and life experiences lacked value or significance, despite the best of intentions.

As an executive coach and racial equity trainer and facilitator . . . I now have more than a dozen years of direct experience with nonprofit leaders who struggle to simultaneously support their own well-being and effectively steward the optimal health and well-being of loved ones, service organizations, boards, and staffers. I have observed and tracked with painstaking detail how cycles of conditioning from a preponderance of socializing forces contributes to disempowering mindsets, attitudes, and behavioral patterns, including rigidity of thought and action, anxiety and fear of failure, disconnection from other people (which presents as competitiveness, hostility, and sometimes myopia), deficit thinking (e.g., perfectionism, cynicism, insecurity), and internalized beliefs of low self-worth.

As chief executive officer for Grantmakers for Effective Organizations... I have experienced how hierarchical organizational models inherently present barriers to free-flowing enterprise-wide communication, experimentation, and shared decision-making. Due to well-established business practices—plus institutional orthodoxy that prioritizes efficiency and achieving results over high-quality learning and growth experiences for people within workplaces—contemporary organizational dynamics tend to be characterized by distrust, resentment, and, ultimately, suboptimal productivity levels.

Based on experiences from each phase of my career in the nonprofit sector, I can see Gabriela gets it right when she points out the dehumanizing impacts of patriarchy, power hoarding, and unchecked privilege (apportionment of access to opportunity and resources). By sharing the many personal stories of women of color leaders—from visceral accounts of disappointment, betrayal, and unmet expectations to examples of hope-filled aspirations for an equitable service sector—Gabriela gives us clear evidence for why imagining different ways of working together is necessary for the next generation of leaders and professionals to thrive. By challenging us to commit to practice—to free ourselves from the psychological and structural constraints of entrenched habitual patterns— she invites us to dream and experiment our way into new territory for learning, where we have possibilities for mutually gratifying ways of being in community, governing, and structuring our institutions for transformative impact.

Perhaps most importantly, Gabriela helps us see that responding with vigor to the pleas of women of color leaders now creates conditions for all of us to thrive together.

MARCUS F. WALTON
President and CEO, Grantmakers
for Effective Organizations

Preface

*And if living unapologetically is a rebellion,
then joy itself is a rebellion.*

**—JADE CHANG,
"How to Center Your Own Story,"
in *The Good Immigrant***

During the COVID-19 pandemic, as my children repeatedly told me, time lost its meaning. The first two years of the pandemic were full of pain, loss, and disarray on a global, personal, and existential level. The events of 2020, rising across the planet to demand that we all see the injustices and violence in plain sight, contributed significantly to the words in this book flowing out of me like a geyser. Approaching the midcentury mark of my life played a role, as did working as an organization's first executive director of color. These intersecting identities and experiences kept the daily realities of race, leadership, power, belonging, and the need for healing at the forefront. During this time, I intentionally gave myself space to heal—to bring back to center parts of myself I had compartmentalized or shut down, some since childhood.

One memory comes vividly: I close my eyes and hear my extended family and neighborhood friends' voices—in my first home, in Lima, Peru.

In the warm, sweet mayhem of my childhood home, unfastened laughter floats freely—the kind of laughter you let out among close friends and in safe spaces. Voices arguing and talking on top of each other; adults herding children out of the living room.

This is my birthday party. I am six years old. I love birthdays, one day each year to celebrate the simple fact of being alive, a ritual connected to the movement of our planet around the sun. And in my household, guaranteed chocolate cake made by mi mamá and lemon meringue pie made by my madrina, Marisol. There is always fresh cancha (popcorn) and gelatina (Jell-O) in tiny cups at our birthday parties, along with a couple of glass one-liter soda bottles. I can smell the chicha morada my mom is making, a drink made by boiling dried purple corn with spices and fruit rinds.

Sometime in the early evening, as the party's energy reaches its peak, the boys and the older sister of one of the boys lock the wood and glass door between the kitchen and the small patio and take the entire patio for themselves. I am so angry and filled with a pulsating determination.

Vamos! I lead the pack of little girls as we march up to the glass door that separates the steamy kitchen—smelling sweet and salty and like chicha morada—from the coveted patio space, where the highly prized metal swing set my parents had recently purchased awaits us—or would if the patio hadn't been commandeered.

With our small hands balled into fists, we rap on the glass door and demand they let us onto the patio, but the boys and older girl yell "No!" and continue their taunting and laughing—"Jaja, no pueden." As my chest expands, my breathing gets faster and faster, and my brain blinks in search of ideas. The adrenaline feeds my courage, surging from my belly. Before I thoroughly think through the consequences, I punch through one of the glass squares of the kitchen door, scattering shards of glass everywhere.

Now I can reach through the newly made access and unlock the barrel bolt on the other side of the door. I push the door open, and a mass of little girls rush in and climb on the swing set. Before joining the others on the swing set, I walk right up to the boy who led the lock-the-girls-out-of-the-patio expedition. Filled with righteous rage, I stand as tall as I can, leaning into his space, maybe wanting an explanation or an acknowledgment that what he'd done was wrong, but whatever my reason for doing it, I remember the feeling of it: energy dancing through my body, in my belly, tickling my chest, then in the center of my forehead, while my feet hold me firmly on the ground, rooted.

I was claiming my power and using it in service of six-year-old justice. The boy was provoking my actions, but the feeling of not being allowed in was always around me, telling me how to be, how not to be, what to believe (even if it countered reason and simple powers of observation), what to want, what was valuable, how to feel. Although I felt emotionally safe and mostly free to be myself at my family home, Peru in the late 1970s and 1980s was a complicated, violent, unjust, beautiful, scary, and unpredictable place. All around me, the giant metropolis of Lima (and the broader context of Peru) wore its violent colonial past, and attendant racialized power and self-destruction, its rigid patriarchal corset, and Euro-Catholic, Indigenous, and Afro-Peruvian cultures and beliefs, draped alongside the deep and long relationship of its peoples and its lands—the costa, sierra, and selva—in bright display and vibrant flavors. I grew up with terrorist attacks on the news every night, bombs and kidnappings, shortages (of staples, water, electricity), military curfews, and so much violence. I grew up in a beautiful country with a complicated history. A country with so much hurt, I could feel it rising from the ground. I've learned from personal and shared experiences that places hold our collective memories, and they seep into the culture, the people, the soil, the water, and the air, making our ancestral pain and love palpable across time.

At age six, I felt fully me, in alignment with my sense of fairness. I don't recall my parents talking much about justice, yet their three children's personal and professional lives are closely intertwined with social and economic justice issues. Despite our being raised in a fairly gendered way, justice was clearly a value my parents embedded in our lives.

I don't remember many details once the adults came into the patio to check on the sounds of broken glass. I remember all the kids playing on the patio and the swing set for the rest of the evening. It felt full and right. The glass door would not keep us out tonight.

I am grateful for the tiny and, by now, barely visible scar on the side of my wrist. It reminds me of who I am and that we can and should shatter unjust barriers for ourselves and others.

There is a reason this memory is so seared into my increasingly forgetful brain. That act was unapologetically me. At that moment, I acted in service of what I understood as my sense of justice and love for myself and those around me. It was about rejecting exclusion, claiming the commons (swing set!) as a space for everyone; it was about not letting someone else say who could and could not have access (and fun!).

In sharing the stories and reflections in *What Your Comfort Costs Us*, I am punching through a much larger square of the glass door that keeps me and other women of color from claiming our fully embodied power in our lives, communities, and workplaces.

During one of my occasional nocturnal free-writing sessions, the words *your comfort is killing me* came from within in a deeply guttural and visceral way. The words draw a straight line between the comfort of the dominant patriarchal, white-supremacy culture and the harm I and other women of color have experienced in the workplace: these are causally connected and must be addressed that way.

As someone with extensive public health training, I look for the roots of injury and disease and seek ways to prevent further harm, or at least mitigate harm in some way, for myself and others. In *What Your Comfort Costs Us*, I name the harm caused by dominant workplace cultures, structures, and narrow leadership concepts. I invite us to learn from the transformational leadership of women of color, to sit with the constructive discomfort that deep empathy can enable, and to work collectively to transform our workplace cultures.

To heal from the pain, we must first be willing and able to see the harm, empathize with the pain, sit with the discomfort, and not succumb to the very American tendency to jump straight to quick-fix solutions. Because as bell hooks says, "True resistance begins with people confronting pain . . . and wanting to do something to change it."[1]

I found myself nodding energetically as I read Ruchika Tulshyan's words in *Inclusion on Purpose*: "If you have not had lived experiences of racism, it can be more comfortable to live in denial that it exists. That's precisely why we need more white people to sit with this discomfort and investigate how racism impacts the lives and careers of people of color, particularly women of color. It's not easy nor intuitive, but cultivating awareness and empathy is deeply important to inclusive leadership."[2]

This book is part of my contribution to our collective work of cultivating awareness and empathy. As I share stories of how racism has affected my life and career, and those of the many women of color leaders whom I interviewed and surveyed for this book, consider yourself invited to lean into constructive discomfort and refuse the urge to turn away or rest in denial—particularly if you have not lived experiences of racism. If these stories resonate with your own lived experiences, know that you are part of a strong and growing movement to disrupt the unjust status quo of unwell and unsustainable workplace culture.

In writing this book, I recognize that *healing is a collective act*. As I explain in what follows, I reject the notion of the hero or savior leader in our professional and personal lives. At work, healing must be a collective and shared effort, and in our personal lives, it must include those with whom we share space and love.

I am privileged that while writing this book I have had access to various forms of support that have helped me dive deeper into workplace harm while being held in relative safety by a loving network of helpers. I worked with a therapist (a white woman) who accompanied me through a deepened exploration of how to heal and become more fully internally aligned and integrated, helping me recognize that workplace trauma is layered on top of and parasitically feeding upon childhood and other societal and personal traumas. During portions of the writing, I also worked with an executive coach (the brilliant Estrella Dawson), generating a safe space to explore leadership issues using an emotional intelligence framework.

More broadly, the love of family and friends has made acknowledging this harm and working to heal from it tolerable and even therapeutic. The safety of my home and my intimate relationships has been critical to my ability to overcome and work toward healing from workplace abuse and trauma. This network of support is essential to my ability to delve into harms I've experienced, to my active listening to workplace traumas of other women of color, and to my ability to take the pain and cook it up into something I hope to serve to others for nourishment and part of a balanced diet for learning and healing. So proceed with an awareness of how reading the words on these pages lands on you, care for yourself, ask for help, know you're seen, believe you're heard, and *love yourself.*

What Your Comfort Costs Us foregrounds the stories of women of color to disrupt the entrenched white-supremacist and patriarchal structures of workplace cultures that dominate our institutions, and it addresses the need for constructive discomfort and systemic change.* It centers on stories about power, the difference between comfort and safety, the need to take up space, identity and self-determination, fear, our relationship with uncertainty, and the necessary messiness at the heart of change. Ideas about changing workplace culture are spread throughout, along with

---

* I speak of women of color not to dismiss experiences of men of color or trans or nonbinary individuals, but because, while extremely broad, it is a category I belong to. I've talked to many Black, Latine, bi- and multi-racial, Indigenous, and Asian American women about this topic and read reports and articles about women of color experiences in the workplace, so I feel most capable of speaking *about* this very broad, nonhomogeneous group. Nonetheless, I speak only *for* myself.

statistics, research literature, concepts, approaches, and models to explore and inform our work of healing and creating truly safe spaces of belonging.

I share my stories as a step in making myself whole again by purging that which no longer serves me or is toxic to my being. I share it to make my six-year-old self proud. I also write this book because, at my core, I have always believed that when presented with the chance to prevent suffering and mitigate cruelty, one *must* take it. No matter how uncomfortable or scary, when one has eyes on a path away from the needless suffering surrounding us, I believe it is one's duty to light the way and make the path visible for others.

This book asks us to consider how those of us operating in liminal spaces, described by Cyndi Suarez as a space "outside of the status quo" and the "source of new culture," can transform the workplace.[3]

Changing workplace culture requires working at the structural and interpersonal levels, including shifting how we understand, support, and invest in leadership. Working on culture change also means abandoning the obsession with perfection, quantification, and certainty. White supremacy and patriarchy are the air we all breathe, and our workplace institutions are built from the blueprints of white supremacy, patriarchy, and racial capitalism. Throughout this book, I reference these systems of oppression, so let me be explicit about what I mean:

> **White supremacy:** A self-perpetuating system of exploitation, extraction, and oppression that violently imposes the belief that white people and whiteness are superior to non-white people and non-white cultures; it is enforced and propagated by institutions, cultural practices, and power structures that privilege white people socially, politically, and economically. Alternatively, Robin DiAngelo defines white supremacy as a "sociopolitical economic system of domination based on racial categories that benefit those defined and perceived as white. This system rests on the historical and current accumulation of structural power that privileges, centralizes, and elevates white people."[4]

Patriarchy: Patriarchy is a system of relationships, beliefs, and values embedded in political, social, and economic systems that structure gender inequality between those presenting as men and those presenting as women.[5] Attributes seen as "feminine" or pertaining to women are undervalued, while characteristics regarded as "masculine" or related to men are privileged.

Racial capitalism: Introduced by political scientist Cedric J. Robinson, racial capitalism is a framework that recognizes the intersection and dependency between capitalism and racism and the racialized commodification of humans.[6]

Because U.S. society is built upon these cultural systems, the growing demographic diversity alone is not enough to create cultural and psychological safety for everyone in our society and workplaces. Increasing diversity without inclusion, belonging, or safety is causing women of color real and cumulative harm. I fear that if we continue to accept this, willingly or not, the damage to our society will be irreparable.

But I believe a different way is possible. I believe we have what it takes to create a future not yet imagined, one that engages with the genuine existential crises of our time and responds with care, courage, curiosity, and creativity.

This book does not offer a step-by-step recipe for fixing workplace culture. There is no such recipe. I share our stories and insights and deliver lessons and information to build your capacity to engage with effective workplace culture change. I offer an opportunity to truly recognize, sit with, and move toward understanding the experiences, perspectives, and courage of women of color leaders working to create a safer world for *all* of us.

Culture work is messy, and it is anything but linear. It isn't apparent and requires a multiplicity of sensing and knowing—conditions that women of color, by necessity, are particularly adept at navigating. As you read this book, I invite you to not turn away from uncomfortable realities and truths. Push beyond your discomfort to make space for the possibility of a different way. I invite you to sit with and process the truths in this book to take a conscious step toward acknowledging and transforming our currently unwell workplace culture.

I hope the truths shared through these pages will move and inform you and inspire you to abandon the supremacist and racist, the race-neutral, and the colorblind poison apples we've been forced to feed on so far. The lessons from the stories shared on these pages can bring us closer to co-creating workplaces and leadership models built on values that foster care, health, dignity, respect, and growth through solidarity-based, anti-racist approaches. As you read these stories, give them space and hold them lightly, and maybe we can start healing together.

Presumed Audience

In bringing together the unprocessed ingredients for this book and turning them into what I hope will be a nourishing meal for the soul, I had to ask myself, *Who am I cooking for?*

This book is written in unapologetic solidarity with other women of color—solidarity with my sisters, friends, and colleagues who have shared their stories and listened without judgment to mine. And to the women of color reading this book: You are seen and valued; I hear and believe you. Thank you for working to create a new and safer world for us all.

The women of color reading this book already know these stories; they *live* them. Part of how we support each other is by witnessing each other's stories, by knowing that they collectively show the need and path for transformative change. Although I wrote this book to give voice to my and other women of color's experiences as workplace leaders, it is clear to me now that the audience is not only women of color. This book is for all people in positions that shape, challenge, and change workplace cultures. In the U.S., this is disproportionately people who identify as white. Institutional leaders, organizational decision-makers, boards, executive and management staff, organizational consultants, educators, human resources, recruiters, and funders, this book is written for you, *especially if you identify as white or benefit from the structures of whiteness.*

If you are a white person in a position of power, you need to read this book.

Acknowledgments

This book would not be possible without the candor and generous sharing of the women I spoke to and surveyed for this project. While this book is written through my specific vantage point and perspective, I have contextualized and broadened my perspective with primary and secondary research, including the stories and insights gathered through interviews with ten change-making leaders (who identify as Black, Latine, Asian American, biracial, and immigrant women) in 2022 and early 2023 and input gathered from thirty-two women of color across the U.S. (who identify as African American, Black, Latine, Asian American, Indigenous/ Native American, multiracial, immigrant, and Middle Eastern) through an open-ended survey in 2023. I feel such deep gratitude for every single woman who shared with me for their trust, courage, and culture-shifting leadership. My respect for and solidarity with women of color leaders, like those I surveyed and interviewed, made writing this book irrepressible and necessary. *Thank you.*

I wrote this book while working full-time as the first CEO of color at a private independent foundation in a predominantly white state to which we had just moved and where we had no family or community, and with the COVID-19 pandemic as the constant backdrop. I felt the need to respond to the state of the world with deep love and try to bring all of me to everything I did: as change agent, mother, partner, sister, daughter, friend, and mentor.

Being all of me while navigating uncertainty and leading culture change during that particular time and space demanded a lot. It would have been impossible to conceive of and write this book without the love, care, and partnership of my husband, Rob, and my sons, Nico and Lucas, who gave me space and support and listened patiently to ideas as I spent weekends and evenings sitting on the sofa in our family room reading and typing away.

During the height of the pandemic and the writing of this book, (like so many others) our home became a bubble that at times felt like refuge and, at others, confinement. My sons had just started a new school in a new state when the world shut down, and I can't pretend to fully comprehend how challenging that was for them as teenagers. I remain humbled by their adaptability, grace, and care and will always treasure the closeness we enjoyed during those difficult times. I can honestly say that I have learned (and continue to learn) more about myself, about love, and about humanity from raising my sons than any other source. Gracias, mis amores.

My husband embodied active listening and true partnership as we navigated the pandemic with our kids (and part of the time with his mother) and multiple dogs and a cat in a place we had moved to for my job, just a few months before COVID-19 changed it all. Rob held steady, lovingly, as I rode the roller coaster of being an immigrant woman of color leader in predominantly white spaces and he embarked on a new profession as a therapist. At times, his relentless belief in me as a leader was the bridge I needed while wading through choppy waters to own and embody my power. We somehow managed to remain a loving community within our home; all four of us intentionally contributed to taking care of ourselves and each other, even when we (as we all inevitably do) tripped over ourselves, needed more than gave, or acted an ass. My family during the pandemic was my greatest embodied experience in shared emergent leadership and interdependent community, rooted in love.

Outside the protective bubble of our home, my sister has always provided me sister-friend love, accompaniment, and solidarity (while being the most wonderful sister anyone could hope for). She modeled courageous and brilliant workplace leadership and excellence in writing while juggling her multitude of personal and professional roles and obligations. My parents' unwavering belief in me and excitement about my book project felt like a warm embrace, especially during the long months we were continents apart and could not see each other due to COVID. Their undeterred sense of adventure, curiosity, and commitment to family and the common good significantly shaped the architecture of who I am. My brother showed me that work is not life and life should not be all about work. After working for a global organization where he seemed to be perpetually on call during the pandemic, he left a high-status, well-paying job for a better quality of life and a lower-paying job. I admire, and seek to learn from him, the way he has kept the things that bring him joy (music!) central in his life. While writing this book, during the harsh uncertainty of pandemic times, I was deeply aware of how fortunate the five of us in my family of origin are to have each other (and our growing family branches), to have an unconditional grounding of love with people who put ethics, compassion, and curiosity above competition, self-interest, and apathy. We're a quirky lot, and we learn (and unlearn) with and from each other still. Besos!

My community of badass women friends (*you know who you are*) gave me strength, confidence, and soul-filling friendship (and laughs and cries) that countered the deep isolation that the combination of leadership and the pandemic (and long winters) concocted. A special thank you to my friend Carol, who provided a magical space for writing and collective rest with friends and my sister at different stages of writing this book.

As someone who too often has struggled to ask for help, I am deeply grateful for the generosity of time and guidance in reviewing and providing valuable and clarifying feedback on the first draft of the book to: Cyndi Suarez (author, former president and chief editor of *Nonprofit Quarterly*), Yanique Redwood (philanthropic leader, author of *White Women Cry and Call Me Angry*), and Mathina Calliope (author and editor).

Gracias, del corazón.

Introduction

As I meet the half-century mark of my life on this earth, I feel an intensified need to live without pretense and to fully claim my right to live with dignity, "the glue that holds all of our relationships together" and "the mutual recognition of the desire to be seen, heard, listened to, and treated fairly; to be recognized, understood, and to feel safe in the world," as understood by Donna Hicks and explored in her book *Dignity: Its Essential Role in Resolving Conflict.*[1] So I have been pondering deeply: *What can fully realized leadership look like for me?*

As a child, I wanted to be a photographer for *National Geographic* magazine. As an introvert, the role of quiet observer suited me well. I certainly never had any desire for leadership. However, an irrepressible drive to live in alignment with my values and to push away from the inherent cruelty of the systems around us has made me take on formal and informal leadership roles throughout my life. Speaking up when things are not just has felt inevitable because justice is so possible and the current state so unnecessary.

Engaging in advocacy is not optional for women of color in leadership positions. The issues we work on are fundamental for us; they are *personal.* They are not something we can elect out of (although some may try). As I write this, I am one of under 2 percent of foundation CEOs in the U.S. who identify as Latine (and under 5 percent of foundation board members, so Latine perspectives and experiences are not well represented). Meanwhile, Latinas are about 16 percent of the total female population in the U.S.; by 2050, we will be one out of every four women in the U.S.

In the U.S., most people in leadership positions find themselves facing expectations and assumptions defined by leadership models created for the archetype of white, Christian, individualistic, cisgendered men as the capitalist hero-leaders. These narrow and limited models create unhealthy, unwelcoming situations for those of us who don't fit the parameters of the aforementioned identities and expectations. They also limit the potential of organizations and society. We know from decades of research and embodied experiences that diverse teams are stronger and more creative, and for my part, I commit to

fully and unapologetically embody myself;
To own my strengths and scars
To claim and employ the fullness of my powers
in service to what is possible.

Locating Myself

I show up in the world as
   tall,
      bilingual and bicultural,
         immigrant, and
            strong.
         Mestiza,
           ni de aqui ni de alla,
   filling out my curved body, too familiar with pain.
         Mother, sister, daughter, partner, friend;
            a woman of color shedding my colonized skin.

Despite my confidence and learned comfort with speaking up, despite repeatedly being told that I am intimidating and scary, despite my extensive education, despite my unhealthy level of pain tolerance and pathological patience, I have too often had to make life changes and career moves that, while necessary to my well-being and psychological safety at the time, were not my choice but an act of self-defense.

I have succumbed repeatedly to tunnel vision and letting work be the center of my energy and attention. I have let others' wounds manifest as my pain, taking responsibility for others' discomfort with me. Decades into my life, I am learning (finally) to commit to the practice of marking boundaries for my well-being and, in so doing, contributing to the collective safety of us all in an aspirational future.

Years of talking to women of color friends, meeting women of color at conferences, parties, workshops, and in Zoom rooms, and reading stories of the harm being done to women of color in workplaces have made me realize that my own experiences belong to a broader and all-too-common cultural pestilence that gets filed under "microaggressions," just part of "doing the work," or even professionalism.[2] In too many workplaces, the dignity of women of color is routinely violated and treated as acceptable collateral damage.

Being forced to spend so much time and energy on making the spaces where we work safe distracts and derails energy, creativity, and attention from the real change, the real work of creating a new and safer world for all of us. We who exist at these intersections of gender and race are being abused by the current system. This is concretely why we need to change our workplaces, so that we can stop the harm and the disconnection between our values and visions and our actions and structures; so we can stop using ourselves up to survive, and instead let ourselves get deep into the dreaming and doing; so we can all be safe and thrive.

These experiences of harm rob too many women of color of professional self-determination, health, wealth, and safety and threaten the livelihoods of women of color, their families, and communities. I owe those who harm me nothing but the truth. I need to repeat it over and over:

I owe those who harm me nothing but the truth.
In silence, I fear I become complicit in the practice of fetishizing, extracting from, and abusing women of color.

Conditioned all too effectively to accept and manage pain and maltreat-
    ment as a necessary part of existing.
Fear is never a path to liberation or stepping fully into one's embodied
    power.
I owe those who harm me nothing but the truth.

Truth is a prerequisite to repair and healing. So I share these truths out of love. Love that helps us all grow, evolve, and move beyond our current limitations. I share to draw clear boundaries from now on, as an invitation to speak honestly about harm visited upon anyone who doesn't uphold a supremacist culture, and as a step toward decentering the comfort of those who chose to cause me and so many others harm. I share because I was shaken by a quote from Zora Neal Hurston in the introductory pages of a book I read, *In the Dream House* by Carmen Maria Machado: "If you are silent about your pain, they'll kill you and say you enjoyed it."

The Professional as Personal

Who I am and what I do professionally are directly shaped by my personal life and experiences. I was born in Lima, Peru, a desert megacity on the Pacific coast of South America, in 1973. My childhood memories are marked by Sendero Luminoso (Shining Path, a violent Maoist terrorist group), El Niño current and earthquakes, narco-traficantes, hyperinflation and rapidly changing currencies (soles, intis, nuevo soles), blackouts and water shortages, state-imposed curfews, and seemingly inescapable violence and poverty. The Peru I grew up in was complicated, marred by colonialism and its cruel progeny.

I grew up surrounded by extended family within walking distance. Our lives were shaped by the warm routine of meals and visits with extended family juxtaposed against the chaos and violence of Peruvian society. When I was ten years old, my father left a full-time job that provided our family with a middle-class livelihood to study in the U.S. We moved many times, as my dad received consecutive prestigious scholarships (Fulbright and MacArthur, among others) for his studies at universities in the U.S. and England, and our family of five lived from the scholarship income. Navigating school in England and the U.S. when I didn't speak English was a crash course in emergence and adaptability.

Sometimes when we moved, we would arrive when the school year had already started and leave before it ended—shifting from northern- to southern-hemisphere school calendars and mind-blowingly different cultures and education systems. To make the scholarship funds stretch to cover our family of five, my mom modeled creativity and adaptability to produce a sense of home in every place we lived. I recall watching her transform an empty townhouse into an inviting home by stacking empty milk crates and draping them with decorative blankets and fabrics to serve as furniture while adding color and warmth. Food is love, so my mom improvised with available ingredients to cook the tasty dishes we were used to having in Peru. We spoke only Spanish at home and created an island of our unique brand of Peruvian culture wherever we lived.

My high school years were completed across three countries in three continents. After finishing school a year early (a story for another time), I applied to colleges and did the only financially feasible thing: I went to college where my dad taught, the same as my siblings. After years of moving around and living in different places in different countries, I still thought of myself as a Peruvian living in the U.S. It was only once my children were born in the U.S. that I thought of myself as an immigrant.

As an adult, I have continued to move around, and the concept of home has become more about the people I share my life with than any specific place. While in graduate school, I had planned to work in global health, thinking I'd use my experience with moving and living in different cultures to work internationally, maybe even go back to Peru. But the reality of school loans kept me in the U.S., slowly paying off my debt. Curious about how best to contribute to creating healthy communities, I worked in various sectors to learn from different perspectives. I have worked in nonprofits, a nonpartisan policy organization, academia, local government, as an independent consultant, founding director of a grassroots reproductive justice organization, and institutional philanthropy.

In all the roles I've held in all these sectors, I, like many women of color and immigrants, have felt compelled to overwork, over-function, and hold myself to unrealistic and exhausting standards. All while navigating biases, prejudices, and power dynamics that are invisible to too many.

Education

I am a foreign-born immigrant Latina with master's and doctorate degrees in public health. I name my education when I describe myself because it was hard-earned and not a privilege available to everyone, especially foreign-born Latines in the U.S. As a child, I remember being told by my grandmothers that their fathers did not allow them to finish school. Both matriarchs made it clear that they deeply resented this act of exclusion, which in no way took their desires and capabilities into account. Now, as a Latina in the U.S., I know I belong to a growing and very diverse segment of the population that is undervalued, under-resourced, underpaid, and too often excluded from decision-making and leadership roles.

My maternal grandmother, Cotita, told me she excelled at school and wanted to be a doctor as a child. The nuns at her school spoke to her father about his bright daughter and offered a scholarship so she could study medicine. He turned this down and pulled her out of school before she could finish, tasking her instead with helping at home in the hacienda where they lived in Ancash, in the Andes of Peru. Years later, her younger brother would go on to study medicine. I was a child when Cotita told me that story (numerous times), not fully aware of the social constraints she'd lived with but sensing her heartbreak and bitterness.

Both grandmothers were women of immense fortitude and unabashed intelligence; their presence was felt in every room they entered, and they both powered through barriers and losses in their own, distinct ways.

Both were widowed with decades left to live and had to become primary income earners for themselves and their households quite suddenly. As a granddaughter of Abuela Olga and Mamatita (what my siblings and I called Cotita), I hope that in some way my and their other grand-daughters' educational and professional accomplishments can existentially soothe some of the gendered exclusion they had to endure during their lives.

Maybe not surprisingly, in the first decade of my career, I observed white men and women with bachelor's degrees access leadership positions. Even with a master's degree, I kept being told that some jobs and roles were beyond my preparation. So a decade after getting a master's degree in public health, I returned to a doctoral program while leading a reproductive justice organization and raising my children as a single mother. For four years of graduate work, I pushed myself physically and emotionally as I navigated separation and eventual divorce while living a continent away from my family of origin, except for my sister, who was also living in the U.S.

School and work peers, friends, and family enveloped me and my children in love and support during these challenging years. *Community is at the center of everything.*[3] In 2012 I graduated with a doctoral degree from the University of North Carolina, Chapel Hill. My dissertation focused on the perceived barriers to family planning information and services for foreign-born immigrant Latinas in Kentucky and involved primary, qualitative research. I interviewed care providers, policy workers, and immigrant Latin American women who participated in women's groups run by a Latina-led and -serving community-based organization, La Casita Center. I analyzed their stories to make sense of a complex and complicated system.

Throughout the research, I was seldom surprised, although frequently heartbroken, by the findings. I didn't expect that I would end up writing about the role of funders and how they held power over the scrappy organizations doing their best to serve their communities. My work had often depended on grant funding, and I was familiar with the anxiety of working for soft money. While I spent excessive time explaining, justifying, and running interference with the primary funding intermediary of the reproductive justice work I led, I hadn't given the philanthropic field much thought. What I learned through my research made me both curious and concerned, so I determined to learn more about foundations and their role in the social change ecosystem.

An Outsider Within

It has been over a decade since I started working in institutional philanthropy, and I often wonder how much longer I can stay. In the U.S., just slightly over one-quarter of all foundation staff identify as people of color, and about 10 percent of foundation leadership identify as a person of color. Philanthropy is an overwhelmingly white field. I have felt like an infiltrator in this field, someone who wasn't expected in the leadership seats, someone whose life experiences and leadership approaches are outside the norm. I entered the field with clear intentions to challenge the culture of paternalism, unassailable capitalism, and white supremacy so deep in the bones of philanthropic structures, and to do so lovingly, transparently, and collaboratively.

Both as a grant seeker and grant maker, I have too often witnessed funders' good intentions cause actual harm at worst and, at best, be based on paternalistic, supremacist, Christian, white-savior assumptions and belief systems. I have worked at three foundations in three states, most recently as CEO of a statewide, private, independent foundation working in service of a culture of equity and interconnectedness for the well-being of people, animals, and the environment. While this book is not limited to philanthropy, my experience with and within philanthropy has made robust contributions to what is included here. Further, philanthropy is a useful sector to explore ideas of leadership and organizational culture because funding can drive organizational decisions, strategies, resource availability, and direction in the broader nonprofit sector. The influence of philanthropy is truly oversized, and its impact is felt across sectors.

A Global Moment of Deceleration and Whiplash

We find ourselves in a unique moment globally, locally, and existentially. The COVID-19 pandemic brought our fractured humanity to an uneven halt. As our breakneck speeds decelerated to make sense of what was happening, the vast, deeply embedded injustices came more into focus for those who typically exist without injustice, demanding their daily attention, energy, and dignity. As many who before stood on the sidelines of justice work joined protests and lent their voices to calls asserting that Black Lives Matter, some of us held our breath a little, allowing a modicum of qualified hope that collective empathy might awaken and that solidarity might finally become more than a word.

During this difficult and tragic time for so many across the world, too many people lost loved ones to COVID-19 and racist violence. To some of us, it was a moment of reckoning, a glimpse of recognition that our systems aren't broken; *they work precisely in the cruel way they are intended to* (more on this later in the book). Public health—a field based on the belief in collective good and shared responsibility—was barely functional as governments in the U.S. (and other nations influenced or coerced by neoliberal policies conceived by wealthier countries and international organizations working in the interest of rich nations and capitalism-as-democracy ideologies) fumbled through diluted, contradictory, short-sighted, disorganized messaging and nonpolicies, and *it showed.*

We should've been better prepared for the pandemic, we should've been able to prevent the worst of it, we should've been able to protect the lives of the many millions who died, of the countless children made orphans—and we didn't, because of intentional decisions our chosen leaders have made for decades. For centuries. We are still, and for the foreseeable future will be, dealing with the consequences of this.

With the global ideological emperor showing its ass, many people lifted their eyes to see the mess we call modern society. The disruption to daily grinds allowed many to realize that the dogma of rugged individualism and pulling yourself by tattered bootstraps was never going to undo the nested supremacist systems of oppression that benefit a capitalist few and exploit most others (including our planetary home). The catastrophic level of preventable deaths from global and racial inequities in the pandemic's impact was not accidental or natural. It resulted from multipronged and intentional decisions made over a very long time for the sake of ideological imperialism, life as warfare, winning as purpose, supremacist exclusion, genocide as a tactical choice, and violence as humanity's crutch.

Our disconnection might look like reasonable self-interest when considered on an individual basis. But seemingly mundane inequities add up to colossal cruelty because supremacy does not limit itself; no boundary is uncrossed or unclaimed. Our societal brokenness feels unambiguous to me when I look at the values implicit in our collective actions over the past hundreds of years. Let me be clear: white supremacy is not accidental or natural, and supremacist cultures are not inevitable or necessary.

A Word about Truth-Telling, Rage, and Comfort

The stories shared in this book are real; they are windows into experiences you may recognize or could never imagine happening to you. These stories are drawn from my own experiences and those of the over forty women of color leaders who contributed theirs to this book. I conducted in-depth interviews with ten women of color leaders and surveyed over thirty women of color in leadership positions across the United States who work in nonprofit, philanthropy, and higher education. The stories shared on these pages are true, but I have changed all names and identifying information to minimize risk to those who shared their stories of workplace abuse.

Like many, I want to live and work in a society with ethical and accountable institutions. Yet the cost of working is disproportionately high for women of color (who earn significantly less than white men or women). Although individuals delivered the abusive behavior in the stories shared, it was the workplace cultures and structures that allowed—at times encouraged and rewarded—such behavior to take place, and most often without repercussion. I expect us to use our collective experiences to tear down the unjust systems, not tear each other down. (See adrienne maree brown's *We Will Not Cancel Us.*[4])

However, that does not mean these pages have no room for anger. Anger is a normal and healthy reaction to injustice, and as Kristin Neff states in *Fierce Self-Compassion*, "the willingness to get angry is, therefore, a political act as well as a personal act of assertion of our rights."[5] This book, rooted in the experiences and stories of women of color leaders, will challenge many people's sense of comfort. White-supremacy culture coddles the privileged with a belief in a right to comfort.[6] Therefore, voices that speak directly to the injustices and harms caused by a system that feels "normal" to so many will predictably disrupt the comfort of the privileged.

This book offers a way to practice empathy, particularly for white-identifying individuals in positions of organizational and institutional power, who are seldom forced to operate in a culture that is not of them and for them. Hila Mehr says empathy "has a critical role in creating positive social change; it will enable us to become more collaborative and respond more thoughtfully to social issues."[7] May the stories in this book guide you more deeply into the practice of empathy, constructive discomfort, and courage.

How This Book Is Organized

This book is built around the stories of women of color who are leaders in nonprofit, philanthropic, and higher education institutions in the U.S.

I weave our stories into recurring themes and provide analysis and reflections in a section called "What This Experience Can Teach Us" following each story or set of stories. The stories are the heart of this book and serve as vehicles for empathy, growth, and applied learning. I pepper quotes throughout the book, using pseudonyms and a general descriptor, from the women I surveyed and interviewed. I contextualize the stories by sharing facts and statistics about women of color in the workplace. Finally, I explore structures as containers of culture, continuing to bring the voices of the women I spoke to into my analysis. I end this book with hope, offering alternative workplace approaches framed around reflections from the women I interviewed about what a workplace that nurtures our leadership would look and feel like.

I weave my vision for justice throughout the book. Justice that feels like a magnificent unfurling of our collective dreams, seated in the inescapable interconnectedness and interdependence of all living things—past, present, and future. Justice that is dynamic, evolving, and capable of holding tensions and apparent contradictions. Justice that is rooted in love and manifests as solidarity. I hope you will feel its presence on these pages as you find your way into a relationship with justice.

Claiming Space by Telling Our Stories

Our current workplace cultures limit our imagination and our humanity. I offer these stories with courage and vulnerability to give you access to a broader reality. A reality that enables us to work collectively to change the nature, purpose, and values that undergird our current workplace culture and its underlying assumptions about power and leadership. These stories explicitly illustrate, backed by extensive experience and available research, that women of color in leadership experience a unique set of intersecting and harmful treatments that differ from how other leaders are treated:

> *"I think that 100 percent we're treated differently,*
> *and it just shows up in so many different ways."*
>
> —SHANTI, Asian American nonprofit leader

These are stories about power, about the difference between comfort and safety, and about taking up space; these are stories about identity, self-determination, fear, and our relationship with uncertainty, and they are stories about the beautiful messiness in the heart of change. These stories are our songs, loud and without shame, refusing to suffer in silence.

As Elizabeth Leiba states in her book *I'm Not Yelling: A Black Woman's Guide to Navigating the Workplace*, "Sharing our stories peels back that layer of shame that people doing inappropriate behavior count on. When they make us think we're to blame, we internalize what they've done and give them protection to keep doing it repeatedly. By asking others about their experiences and sharing your own, we are often confronted with the reality validated by numerous studies, research, and surveys. This reality is that most of us are enduring the same behavior, and we're suffering in silence!"[1]

1

Understanding the Difference between Safety and Comfort

To create safer environments,
people and circumstances must be transformed.

—MARIAME KABA,
We Do This 'Til We Free Us

Before delving into our stories, let me address a critical distinction: the difference between comfort and safety. For some people, changing workplace culture to be more inclusive of worldviews and leadership approaches beyond those that center white, male, Christian, capitalist, and individualistic identities is interpreted as making white workers feel less welcome, comfortable, or supported. I do believe that individuals who identify with and feel most comfortable in white-dominant culture will feel somewhat or very uncomfortable as culture changes in their workplace. At the same time, for those of us who don't identify with white-supremacy culture but are living and working in institutions dominated by it, we've normalized this discomfort and lack of safety. I, and countless others, propose that we create a more expansive and inclusive mold for workplace culture that no longer favors a narrow band of individuals and perspectives, and instead welcomes a broader spectrum of realities, for our collective benefit.

I often wonder what U.S. society would be like if all white people in the U.S. were allowed to sit in spaces where they are not the majority, where their culture is not the norm. Imagine if people who identify as white had to learn to navigate across unspoken assumptions, code-switching, and anticipating how others might respond to them when they are viewed as *other* or *less than*. If you've never had the experience of being a racial or ethnic minority, I highly recommend you seek this experience out. And not just for an hour at a restaurant (although maybe you can start there), do it for long enough that you feel *uncomfortable*, and then stay longer. White supremacy has deprived most white people in the U.S. of the skills to simultaneously hold multiple views and perspectives, because they don't have to. Being othered builds muscles that the majoritarian population doesn't have to develop, and to their detriment. From a brain science perspective, always being comfortable means that you have less incentive to learn new things.

Safety is necessary for healthy development and growth. Comfort is nice to have, but not necessary, and at times can even be limiting. When discomfort is unfamiliar, it can be confused with a lack of safety. Let me share a little story about the difference between comfort and safety before we delve into the stories of women of color leaders.

In 2012 I ended up in the emergency room with what I feared was a stroke. Earlier that evening I had attended my children's primary school dinner celebration. I ate the dinner the kids prepared with help from their teachers: pasta, garlic bread, salad, and cheesecake. Soon after leaving the event, I started to feel light-headed. By the time I got home, I felt unwell and my mom put the kids to bed (luckily she was visiting). I started to feel tingling all over, my tongue felt large and clumsy, my words were slurring, and I had to sit down for fear I would pass out as my field of vision began to narrow.

Realizing this was only worsening, I enlisted my ex-husband to take me to the emergency room, where I was told I was having an anaphylactic reaction and was asked what I was allergic to. My answer was *nothing*. I've been sensitive to pineapple since childhood, but the worst effect was that my tongue hurt for a day or two after eating pineapple. I was sure I hadn't been exposed to pineapple during the school dinner. This left the ER staff and me baffled.

After a few challenging months of an elimination diet and comprehensive allergy tests, we identified that I had several food allergies, and one, wheat, caused anaphylaxis if not treated immediately. This meant I had to become very proactive and communicative about my needs with food as a matter of life and death. If I consume wheat or even eat something that has had contact with wheat, my blood pressure drops, my breathing becomes depressed, my throat and mouth swell, and my digestive system tries to expel everything.

Since this life-altering development in my life, my experience has been that many people treat my food allergies as a personal affront to their freedom, minimize it, or feel like they're put out if shared meals require accommodations they're not used to. Some people think it is a fad to order gluten-free (the more common and easily understood way to convey my wheat allergy) and treat it with disdain. Although not exposing me to wheat requires more attention, some people *equate their discomfort with my safety.* Having a wheat-free meal, or eating so that no wheat items touch my food, is a necessary accommodation for my safety and survival, and at most, a temporary inconvenience for others (except for my family, who lives with the reality of my food allergies every day).

Similarly, culture change that decenters white dominant culture is a matter of safety for Black, Indigenous, and other people of color, and at most, a discomfort for people most at ease in white dominant culture. Making structural adjustments—such as keeping wheat items separate from my food, paying attention not to pass the bread basket to others over my plate, or asking that the bread be brought in a separate plate from the appetizer we're sharing—is not a threat to anyone else's safety, just their sense of comfort.

After years of dangerous experiences and ER visits, I no longer feel the need to apologize or endanger myself to protect the comfort or convenience of individuals sharing a meal with me. Similarly, I no longer accommodate, protect, or advantage individuals who prefer the familiarity and inherent injustices of white-dominant workplace culture.

My safety, like that of all people of color, is indisputably more important than anyone's comfort. What women of color bring to the table as leaders is worth the discomfort you'll feel as workplace culture changes to accommodate and support various forms of leadership, ways of knowing, and perspectives more inclusively. And you'll still get to eat your bread and share your perspectives, so long as you don't insist on eating your bread over my plate or silencing my voice when it doesn't conform with your viewpoint.

Chronic feelings of lack of safety can take a toll on one's body. Sensing a lack of safety triggers production of cortisol and adrenaline in our body, which can have significant effects on our physical and mental health. To be clear, we are talking about safety in many dimensions. Stories in this book, and those that didn't make it into the book, tell of workplaces lacking psychological and economic safety.

The Center for Creative Leadership provides an excellent overview of psychological safety and its critical role in workplace culture, creative thinking, decreased interpersonal conflict, and higher productivity.[1] I highly recommend you spend some time reading about psychological safety and ways to nurture a culture of psychological safety at work.

> *"And then once we get in the door, we must constantly prove ourselves with all this added judgment and burden from boards that don't trust us and undermine and gaslight us. And then, on top of that, we impose this sense of having to speak for so many more than just myself. That's just the system. That's just its default setting. So, it's the compounding nature of all of that, that makes it so hard, and it's no wonder we get sick. No wonder we're tired. No wonder we quit."*
>
> —ALEJANDRA, Latine philanthropic leader

Navigating psychologically unsafe workplace cultures while leading change takes a toll. As Gail Christopher and Deepa Iyer state in "Honoring and Supporting Women of Color Leaders," "Many women of color leaders, for example, are expected to bring about equity and justice within and outside of their organizations, but do not receive the resources, including funding and team collaboration, they need to create sustainable change."[2] In other words, *I think it requires organizations to be very different from how they have historically been constructed to be, and I think that's scary to the people who have gained power in the current system.*
—ALEJANDRA, Latine philanthropic leader

Throughout this book, you will gain a clearer understanding of the difference between safety and comfort. How exactly is white dominant culture unsafe for women of color? The following stories allow you to safely glimpse and learn from the experiences that I and other women of color leaders have in workplaces across the U.S.

2

Talking about Racism Is Hard

Making women of color responsible for addressing racism in your organization is causing us harm

A nonprofit that had recently made public commitments to racial equity hired, in a short span, multiple staff members of color, mostly women. One of the newer hires, Claudia (a Latine woman), was asked to develop a racial equity workshop with her coworker, Monique (a Black trans woman), and facilitate it for the staff team as part of the organization's racial equity learning. Both tried saying no, intuiting that it was not best practice for staff to lead these workshops for their coworkers. Having to facilitate discussions about race, racism, and equity while navigating gendered and racialized power dynamics at work would put them in a challenging situation and create a lack of psychological safety. It would also make it impossible for them to participate in this organizational learning, because they had to play the role of facilitator. Confidentially, Claudia and Monique shared their fear of the emotional toll it would take on them to conduct a racial equity workshop in a workplace where they both had experienced a barrage of microaggressions.[1] Monique and Claudia got along quite well, so they decided to find a way to co-create a workshop that would contribute something positive to the work culture.

Over the next couple of months, both Monique and Claudia experienced racialized and gendered interactions that heightened their concern about doing the workshop. The workplace dysfunction caused Monique to look for other jobs, and by the time of the workshop, Monique had left the organization. Claudia assumed the workshop would be canceled and made a comment about it to her boss:

"Hey, Andy, without Monique, the workshop won't work, so I'm thinking we should cancel it, and we could maybe find an outside group to come in and do a workshop for all of us." Andy (her middle-aged white male boss) disagreed and replied in his ever-upbeat tone: "Oh my gosh! No, we are so counting on you doing this workshop for us. You told me you could do it; you *have to* do it. It'll be great, don't worry!"

He told Claudia to adapt the workshop and do it by herself. Claudia knew this wasn't a good idea. Still, as her gut turned into knots, she knew, from experience and observation, that pushing back on this request would result in weeks of her boss ignoring her and excluding her from meetings and decision-making. On the day of the workshop, Claudia tried to convince herself she could do this, but in doing so, ignored the frantic voice inside her telling her to protect herself: "*This is stupid; such a bad idea . . . This doesn't feel right. I feel so trapped.*"

She didn't feel she should be leading a workshop about race and racism with her multiracial coworkers and all-white managers. And without a co-facilitator, the dynamics of the workshop would be wildly off— Claudia and Monique had designed the workshop to be led by two people of different racial identities and intentionally set it up so they wouldn't be participants, so they could keep some emotional distance and guide their coworkers through some exercises.

As the workshop kicked off, the energy in the room amped up: Her coworkers, encouraged by the managers, joked that it wasn't fair that Claudia didn't have to participate in the activities. "Well, that's not fair! You're part of the team; you should answer all the questions and be part of the exercises. We'll help you—come on!"

Despite her strong sense that it was not the right thing to do, Claudia had to facilitate and participate in the session concurrently. As the only immigrant and Latine person in the group, her experiences often stood out, and she was asked to explain them to her coworkers. "I don't understand what you mean by that." "Is that the same thing as illegal immigration?" "But we're all just part of the human race and have more in common than different." Claudia felt as if acknowledging that she had a different worldview was enough to prompt defensiveness.

Tracy, one of her white coworkers, tried to ease her discomfort by saying, "I think everyone feels like they belong in some spaces more than others, and everyone worries about their children's safety. I don't see how that is a racial thing; I think it's human."

Tracy's words landed differently on the staff of color than on the white staff members. As the words still hung in the air, Claudia saw her white coworkers nodding and smiling and her coworkers of color holding back any expression as they shared worried glances. The palpable potential for white discomfort prompted two of Claudia's Black coworkers to share some rather painful experiences of racism—maybe to illustrate to Tracy the targeted nature of the harms they'd experienced and softly rebuke Tracy's colorblind assertion. These personal accounts of racism brought emotion and vulnerability into the room, making the whole thing feel totally out of Claudia's control.

By the end of the session, it had gotten heavy, with some people opening up, some crying, and others (including Tracy and Andy) showing a shocking lack of awareness of their privilege. Claudia was surprised by the level of sharing and vulnerability and wondered what impact this would have on the various people at the workshop, especially those who'd shared painful experiences and become vulnerable in a space full of colorblind assertions of "a few bad apples" worldviews, in a space of very pronounced and racialized power dynamics. Claudia felt drained and whiplashed from the experience of being both facilitator and participant. She wanted to leave, lie under a blanket with her cat, and let all the feelings and sensations settle in a safe place.

But she had work to do, so she went to her office and shut the door after her coworkers thanked her for a meaningful experience. Claudia felt something akin to jetlag: bone-deep tired and disoriented. In preparation for an upcoming meeting, she walked past Andy's large corner office. Jocelyn, Andy's assistant (a visibly and perpetually anxious white woman), made a face at Claudia that conveyed embarrassment and said,

"Andy went home. He said he was exhausted from the workshop and needed to go home and lie down for the rest of the day."

Claudia stopped in her steps, her jaw dropping. As she tried to understand what Jocelyn had just shared, she was filled with anger, confusion, outrage, and an almost irrepressible need to cry. All she could muster to say was, "What? He left? Did he say anything about the rest of us?" She knew the answer, of course.

This middle-aged white man used his position of authority and power to practice self-care and offered no one else the same. A few other staff overheard Claudia and Jocelyn talking and walked over. As Jocelyn repeated Andy's whereabouts, Claudia exchanged glances with coworkers, who shook their heads in bewilderment. The message was clear: the staff of color had to, were expected to, navigate through the pain, retraumatization, and microaggressions that transpired in the workshop that was forced on them (and especially on Claudia) and carry out the rest of their workday.

Despite her coworkers' praise for how she managed the session, Claudia didn't feel good about the workshop. She felt used and complicit in the retraumatization of herself and her coworkers of color. Andy showed up the following day and said nothing to Claudia about the workshop. Still, later that day, he sent a widely cc'd message praising the workshop and commenting on how committed the organization was to being anti-racist.

WHAT THIS EXPERIENCE CAN TEACH US

What can I say? This is just straight-up centering white comfort, with a healthy dose of weaponized white tears (*and isn't there almost always a narcissistic white man shedding tears at social justice workshops?*). Inherent in this situation is the assumption that people of color can handle racism and talk about racism more easily, so no special considerations need to be taken. For context, consider that women of color carry a disproportionate burden for diversity, equity, and inclusion (DEI) work in their workplaces, regardless of their actual job role. It should not be the job of women of color to explain racism to white people or to people in power (regardless of their racial identity).

The skewed way the staff were allowed to process the workshop sent strong, implicit messages about centering the comfort of those in power, minding your place, and not asking for more than you already have. All in the service of comforting whiteness, patriarchy, and cushioning supremacy so it remains intact.

From the outside looking in, the organization (and its leadership) could claim commitment to racial equity work (and claim it, it did!). But inside, the way that racial equity work was practiced left staff of color disempowered, drained, and vulnerable. If you see yourself in any of the characters in this story, think about how you can get (or give yourself) support, healing, and safety. If you identify with Andy, think about how you can make sure you don't cause this type of harm to those you come in contact with, and how you can, instead, create space for listening to your staff of color, and for processing and healing for everyone at the organization. If you identify with Tracy or Andy, seek opportunities to learn about white dominant culture and racial equity.

This is not an invitation to feel guilty; white guilt is often paralyzing and unhelpful. Consider it an invitation to do your part toward healing our collective humanity because racism and white supremacy dehumanize everyone, including the Andys and Tracys of the world.

CHAPTER 3

Checking the Boxes

Tokenizing and commodifying women of color causes harm and impedes true reform

I walk into a room, and everyone there is terribly proud of himself because I managed to get to the room.

—JAMES BALDWIN, "The Uses of the Blues"

A big part of my experience in the U.S. has been having white people tell me what they think I am. I am aware that I have often been tokenized to check multiple boxes: woman, immigrant, non-white, and for a few years, single mother.

For many years, it seemed to me that organizations couldn't identify other Latinas among a growing community of Latin American immigrants, because I was invited to join numerous boards, committees, task forces, etc. In many ways I was a safe choice, as I served in leadership positions in local government, higher education, and then at a foundation, so I was seen as familiar and more "mainstream." It seemed that choosing me was easier than doing the work of engaging communities and building relationships with other Latinas; maybe Latinas with heavier accents than me, people with darker skin than me, individuals with less formal education than me.

A clear example is when a former coworker (a white woman who had left the organization before me) told me what happened the day I accepted the job. This story was so uncomfortable to her that she didn't want to burden me with it while I was still working at the organization. The story she shared went something like this:

"Brett (middle-aged white male CEO) came into the conference room where the team was gathered for a staff meeting and shared that you had accepted the job offer and would be starting soon. He shared how excited he was that you were joining the organization but admitted that he was a little disappointed because 'I thought she *checked all the boxes*, but she's actually married to a man.'"

I wasn't the immigrant lesbian of color he thought he'd found.

As my friend shared this story, I almost had to laugh at the absurdity of it. That the leader of an organization known for its commitment to racial equity could be so blatant about tokenizing staff and sharing assumptions about the presumed sexual orientation of job candidates was both obscene and sadly not surprising. Some parts of me wondered if I had been hired because they thought I would "check all the boxes," which fed the sense of imposter syndrome that surfaces from time to time.

Speaking of which, let's talk about *imposter syndrome*. The concept comes from research done by psychologists to define a set of internal feelings and thoughts of inadequacy despite external and knowable accomplishments. White women psychologists studied successful white women in the 1970s, and the concept they identified has become widely used. While I have casually used this term, I recognize the problem with naming my self-doubt and sense of inadequacy as an individual-level psychological experience. For all women, particularly women of color, very real external conditions not only incite the experience of imposter syndrome, but actively feed it through workplace practices and cultures that undervalue, silence, and harm women of color despite their evident accomplishments and contributions.

As Elizabeth Leiba so eloquently tells us throughout her book *I'm Not Yelling*, it isn't that women of color lack confidence or competence or are particularly prone to questioning ourselves; it is that we are *treated as if* we are imposters in white dominant culture workplaces.

As Diya, a South Asian American educational leader, said to me, *"I remember hearing the woman who developed the concept of imposter syndrome at a conference, and she's a white woman. And I love lots about it, and I've thought about imposter syndrome a lot, but this model wasn't working for me. It felt like it was a model made for white women, not for me. Just like so many leadership models and mentorship programs for women, it didn't account for the realities I face as a woman of color."* Indeed, Ruchika Tulshyan and Jodi-Ann Burey have written that "for many women, feeling like an outsider isn't an illusion—it's the result of systemic bias and exclusion." In their article "Stop Telling Women They Have Imposter Syndrome," Tulshyan and Burey echo what I heard from several women I interviewed (and affirm my own experience and beliefs about this issue) by saying:

> The impact of systemic racism, classism, xenophobia, and other biases was categorically absent when the concept of imposter syndrome was developed. Many groups were excluded from the study, namely women of color and people of various income levels, genders, and professional backgrounds.[1]

As an Asian American survey participant said, *"The whole 'imposter syndrome' thing can paint women as the problem, but it is a societal problem."*

WHAT THIS EXPERIENCE CAN TEACH US

This situation illustrates the concept of *racial capitalism*, understood as a process that

> relies upon and reinforces commodification of racial identity, thereby degrading that identity by reducing it to another thing to be bought and sold. Commodification can also foster racial resentment by causing non-white people to feel used or exploited by white people. And the superficial process of assigning value to nonwhiteness within a system of racial capitalism displaces measures that would lead to meaningful social reform.[2]

Or as Shanti, an Asian American nonprofit leader, said, *"Also, this idea, that we are embodying the capitalism that we live in, right?"*

Understanding this story as an all-too-common manifestation of racial capitalism should inform considerations of diversity and inclusion strategies and raise awareness about using technical fixes for what requires adaptive cultural approaches. Kiara, a Black philanthropic leader I interviewed, described how women of color are treated at workplaces as *"celebrating us publicly and annihilating us internally and privately."* Tokenizing and fetishizing certain (often historically disenfranchised) identities is not equity, and this common practice harms the individual and the population(s) they belong to. Whether a mental checklist or a literal one, we cannot checklist or DEI-program our way out of oppression and into equity.

Organizations should not jump into hiring staff who "check their boxes" without also committing to look internally at their organizational culture, the values and assumptions intrinsic in structures and processes, and their leadership's willingness to explore their privilege, racism, and other isms. While Black, Indigenous, and other workers of color should have an active role and voice in anti-racism efforts at work, they do not have the responsibility to explain racism, put their trauma on display to illustrate racism to their white coworkers, or "fix racism" in the organizational culture.

Let me be clear: This is not an excuse for not making your organization more diverse. This is an invitation, a call to action, to work not only on diversity but also on real inclusion, a culture of belonging, and the conditions for equity through deep, honest culture change. It is also an acknowledgment that having good intentions and claiming to be anti-racist is not enough to create an equitable workplace culture. As a Black immigrant survey participant explained:

> *"I have been hurt and faced more racism-sexism from people who believe they are anti-racist. They are so good at seeing racism when it happens at a distance (time, geography, scale), but they are resistant to seeing it close up or believing that 'good' people are racist/sexist.*

*"It is like being in an abusive relationship—'anti-racist' 'woke' white men and women will rave about how fabulous you are, the importance of BIPOC people, the beauty, strength, blah blah blah (insert gushing comment about Dr. King here); they will put you up on a pedestal as a remarkable person **and** then pull you down hard with microaggressions, and denying of ism's, and blatant prejudice and discrimination."*

CHAPTER 4

White People Tell Me Who I Am

White people's assumptions and assertions about the identity of people of color harm women of color and limit their options to those deemed appropriate by the supremacist power structure

How can you group an entire people all together as the same? When a white person suggests something be . . . more Latino, I often ask them to show me what they mean 'cause chances are it's stereotypical as hell. It's what they think a Latinx person is.

—DANI FERNANDEZ, "No Es Suficiente," in *The Good Immigrant*

There have been innumerable times in my life when I have been told "what" I am; having white people explain my identity to me as if they know my life experience and ancestry better than me is just part of living as a non-white person in the U.S. One particularly awkward one was on a board where I'd served for a few months.

During a board meeting, the organization's executive director, Courtney, stated that the board needed to work on diversity. After the meeting, she chatted with me. "Could I ask you to help us recruit diverse board members?"

"Yes, definitely. And one is a starting point," I said lightheartedly, knowing and accepting that there is an unspoken expectation for people of color on staff or boards to help or lead diversity efforts.

"What do you mean?" Courtney said, looking perplexed.

Genuinely confused: "Well, me," I said. "Your Peruvian board member."

"Oh, but you're not a real Latina." *She didn't even hesitate.* "I'm talking about Hispanic and African American board members."

I laughed nervously, wanting to disappear, to not be in that absurd situation. I'd had some version of this conversation before and didn't want to have it again. "What do you mean?" I muttered.

Now she fumbled, trying to explain herself, aware that something had changed my emotional state but not aware enough to know why or assume any responsibility. Something to the effect of, "Well, you know, you're not who people think of when they hear Latina. I mean . . . well, you know what I mean. Come on!" Her assumptions seemed so evident that she couldn't explain them to me.

At the same time that she didn't think I was a "real Latina," she did not consider me white or treat me as she treated the white board members. For example, she skipped over me when naming board members who had recently received a community award—even though I was one of three board members who received the award and the first immigrant and Latina awarded; she asked me to take on extra work that I didn't see her asking other board members to take on; she spoke in a much more informal and non-deferential tone with me, etc.

Her assumptions took me back to my experience as a teenager, during the year my family lived on the outskirts of Cambridge, England. The fact that I spoke with a somewhat American accent confused my classmates and teachers, so I periodically had to clarify that I was Peruvian but had lived in the U.S. for a few years and therefore had somewhat of an American accent. Someone I considered a friend at school argued that there was no way I could be Peruvian. "Peruvians," he said, "are short, dark, ugly, smelly people. They're ignorant." I was generically exotic and foreign to my friend but couldn't be specifically Peruvian as it countered his beliefs. I felt a blow that captured my breath. I was horrified, embarrassed on behalf of my friend, embarrassed I had thought him my friend, angry, ashamed, and indignant; it confirmed that I did not belong—not here and not to the stereotypes held by those I considered friends.

Serving on a board, I didn't think I would have to explain to other adults that defining other people's identity for them is inappropriate—and central to supremacist structures. In both instances, there was an implication that my height (I am unusually tall for Peru), education, and "acceptable" accent made me more palatable to white sensibilities. In both cases, I wondered if the white person speaking to me thought they were gracing me with a compliment by implying that I seemed less Peruvian to them than their stereotypes of Peruvians or Latinas. *Racism wears many masks.*

I can't pretend to understand Courtney's intentions or rationale in believing it was acceptable for her to say what she said to me. Still, it inserted doubt into our relationship and undermined trust in her leadership and her ability to see or hear me or anyone she saw as other.[1] She privileged her stereotypes about me over my self-identification, experience, and facts. Having my identity denied by the leadership of an organization where I volunteered left me with a profound sense of powerlessness, invisibility, and not belonging, a reminder that white supremacy is everywhere.

Alejandra: Assumptions That Shape How We See the World

"And as you're being forced to be made small, you start internalizing that, and you forget all of the things you've done in the past."

—SHANTI, Asian American nonprofit leader

One of the women I interviewed shared this story, a different take on white people telling a woman of color who she is.

Alejandra, the executive director of an organization at the time of this incident, served on the board of a national organization and attended the organization's annual conference at a fancy hotel.

Alejandra was sitting in the hotel lobby, dressed in a suit and wearing a conference lanyard around her neck, with a couple dozen other people hanging around between conference sessions. Alejandra was aware that she was the only woman of color here, as is often the case in these leadership spaces.

"Excuse me," a random person approached Alejandra and interrupted her while she was reading, "Could you . . ."

Alejandra didn't remember the precise words the person spoke to her. She was being asked to do housekeeping by a stranger as she sat in the hotel lobby, minding her business as she took a break between conference sessions.

As upsetting as this experience was, it was unfortunately not the first time she'd been presumed to be "the help" by a white person at a professional event. She shared that since her first professional job until now, as ED of an organization and board member of a national organization, people have approached her, even while in the restroom, and asked her to empty the trash, clean the room, pick up dishes, and call housekeeping.

"People see a Brown woman at a hotel or restaurant and immediately go to, oh, this is Maria, the helper, or whatever; it's just astonishing," Alejandra said. "And it's not like I'm sitting there wearing a maid's outfit, right? I'm sitting in a business suit with a lanyard on of a conference when these things have happened to me. And throughout my career and in different states, from California to the South to the East Coast, it has been everywhere. And the assumptions, right? *That I shouldn't even be there.* Let alone that I am with an organization or a leader of an organization, right?"

WHAT THIS EXPERIENCE CAN TEACH US

Supremacist cultures like to define the identity of others and enforce that taxonomy to a degree of absurdity. Supremacy defines who has value and who does not, and changes that category as it sees necessary to maintain power structures and dynamics. I invite you to read about *divide and conquer* tactics in U.S. history, and the evolving nature of who is considered white in the U.S., and you'll see this approach perfected to serve the maintenance of power in the hands of the few.

When I was called "not a real Latina," I was young, early in my career; it was my first time serving on a board, and this experience took me aback. This strange interaction made it clear that my identity, which I had assumed was not up for debate, could be used, erased, or delegitimized by a well-intentioned (and liberal) white leader. It was one of many times I'd realize that regardless of my experience, identity, or reality, those in power would get to assign to me whatever category suited their worldview and comfort.

Denying someone's identity is a violence of erasure; to me, it felt like a taking of my self-determination and stealing my true name. The power felt arbitrary, capricious, entitled, and lacking self-awareness. Some might say, is this such a big deal? And maybe, if this were the only time this had happened, if this story were an oddity, it might seem absurd, silly. The fact that this happens so many times to so many women of color transforms it from a paper cut to a chronic injury. A multiracial woman shared the following through the survey:

> *"There are still so few WOC in positions of power that it's unexpected, and sometimes openly unwelcome to have me in these leadership spaces. But often, it's the unconscious bias of others that's hardest to deal with. Like when I go to a lecture hall to speak, and someone hands me the trash to take out—that's a person who doesn't conceive of a Black or Brown person as the speaker, they must be the help. When a white male colleague tries to build me up by 'supporting me,' talking about how they've looked at my work and approved it, how I meet their expectations— setting me up as their sidekick rather than shutting up and not taking up space—I can speak for myself, and it [their behavior] undermines me!"*

Self-determination is essential to our collective liberation; supremacy defines categories of people in variable ways but always to serve and preference those in power. In this way, supremacy is self-perpetuating, adaptive, and coercive, so we must be intentional and explicit about not allowing the exclusion, suppression, or marginalization of any group or their ability to self-identify and self-name. This experience, and others like it, taught me that identity is complex, nuanced, and necessarily personal. Pay attention to your organizational culture and structures. How can individuals or groups self-identify and speak for themselves? Is it safe to do so?

Are these experiences you can relate to? Or something you couldn't imagine? Have you ever witnessed anything like what Alejandra or I experienced? What does this type of experience say about how our society is organized that there is such a racialized assumption about who works in housekeeping? In leadership? Despite clear markers (wearing a business suit, having a conference lanyard around her neck), white-presenting individuals repeatedly approached Alejandra, an organizational leader, and asked her to take care of their needs. Awareness that this happens to Black and Brown women in the U.S., including at the highest levels of executive leadership, is necessary to change our toxic workplace cultures.

Take a pause and imagine these stories happening around you. Be witness to these stories, and don't turn away from the discomfort they cause you. Use them to build empathy and a worldview beyond your personal experience.

CHAPTER 5

(Invisible) Structural Barriers to Leadership and Leadership Resources

When systems are designed for a specific type of user, anyone outside that type will encounter barriers, and those the system was designed for will rise to leadership and find it nearly impossible to recognize the barriers

As a woman of color, the truth I learned through my own experience and that of the more than 500 women of color leaders I interviewed is that by the time many of us make it to positions of power, we don't feel more empowered; we feel powerless. After a lifetime of over-functioning and overperforming, we end up disconnected, hypercritical of ourselves, and unable to lead from a place of authenticity and vision. We don't feel triumphant; instead, we feel stifled, isolated, and under extreme pressure.

—DEEPA PURUSHOTHAMAN, "Stop Telling Young Women of Color to Accept a Broken System," *Harvard Business Review*

Among the women I interviewed for this book, there was a common perception that advanced degrees were necessary to navigate the many intersecting barriers of sexism and racism. Krista, a Black nonprofit leader who was pursuing a doctoral degree at the time, said, *"I'm going to school to prove who I am. What I already am. I love learning and being with other people who want to learn, but I am doing it to manage the power dynamics in our systems and not because I felt that I was missing something."*

I took a nonlinear path to education. After college, I worked for a few years, then attended graduate school, taking the maximum allowable credits per semester (between seventeen and nineteen because I realized the school charged me the same whether I took fifteen or nineteen credits!) while working part-time to limit the debt I incurred. I worked for ten years and decided that a doctoral degree might open opportunities that seemed to be closed to me with "only" a master's, despite many white people with college degrees accessing them.

I researched doctoral programs that fit both my interests and my life situation. I found a program for mid-career working professionals. At the time, I was leading a grassroots reproductive justice entity I had recently started. To make the funding work (including providing what seemed like fair wages to the community organizers working with me) and to provide flexibility in my personal life as a single mother of two young children, I was paid for thirty hours per week for my full-time work (which was regularly over forty hours, but not during regular business hours).

After applying and interviewing for the doctoral program, I learned that the program defined full-time work as forty hours per week (something that was assumed to be a given, as it was not included in the application information). The necessary adaptation in my work disqualified me from being eligible for the doctoral program I had applied to. Thankfully, the program director recognized the absurdity and invited me to write a letter explaining why this eligibility limitation in the program was inequitable—*one more task for me after my kids fell asleep.*

I persuaded the university program to waive this rigid and exclusionary criterion to the executive leadership doctoral program and was invited in. The next few years were marked by deep learning and support among my peers and professors, but it took a while for me to shake the uneasiness awakened by having to justify my right to a place in the program.

Another example of structural barriers comes from Emilia, a Latine educational leader:

> "I was one of two finalists for a job, and I felt good about it. The interviews went really well, and I thought it was a sure thing. I had extensive work experience, education, and two other [job] offers. So I was taken aback when they offered the job to the other finalist, a white woman from an Ivy League university with no work experience and no job offers.
>
> "When they called me, they asked me to wait a few days [before responding to other job offers] while they worked out a way to hire me as a diversity hire. They ended up hiring both of us, but I had to wait four days while the white woman with the same education, no work experience, and no other job offers didn't have to go through the extra steps, the uncertainty, or being put in a box: I was a diversity hire."

Although Emilia got the job and worked at that organization for several years, the anxiety of waiting extra days and risking losing her other job offers was a deeply racialized experience that the white woman with no work experience didn't have to go through. She also shared that she spent her time at the organization deeply aware that the organization had referred to her as a "diversity hire," which, to some, implied that she somehow lacked what "regular" hires had.

These structural barriers are sometimes so self-enforcing that there is no place to go to challenge the process or decisions. Krista's story illustrates this all too well:

> "I applied for this new position at the place where I'd been working and was told I didn't have enough leadership experience for the new position.

Soon after, another Black woman I knew applied for the position and was also turned down.

"The next thing I knew, a white woman I was supervising in my current role applied, and she got the job! Even though the white woman had no supervisory experience, had less work experience and less education than me, and the white woman had been part of the interviewing team, part of the process that interviewed me and the other Black woman who applied!

"So now the entire leadership team was white women."

WHAT THIS EXPERIENCE CAN TEACH US

These stories provide a few examples of the types of institutional barriers that women of color face in the workplace. Under the guise of *professionalism*—described as a racist construct by Monique Judge and often misused in place of experience—narrow and exclusionary criteria and policies are developed and implemented by organizational leaders and HR departments.[1] For example, leadership is narrowly defined to fit individuals who work forty hours per week in traditional U.S. workplaces. How often do women of color face unnamed and invisible barriers and assumptions as to what a leader looks like? How frequently are our disproportionate familial and community obligations used to keep us from entering spaces of further learning, resources, mentorship, and experience? How often do women of color have to take extra steps, use additional resources, and shoulder additional emotional labor to gain opportunities?

Given the overrepresentation of women of color in informal work sectors, and the unequal burden women carry in parenting and caring for elderly family members, how often are women in general and women of color, specifically, excluded and not even considered for leadership programs and resources? How often are we asked to, forced to, advocate for ourselves above and beyond what our white and male peers must?

Many of the women I interviewed for this book talked about the lack of mentorship opportunities for them. Lack of mentorship is a serious barrier: research indicates that those who experience mentorship "per-form better, advance in their careers faster, and even experience more work-life satisfaction."[2] Many named the absence of women of color mentors in their careers as a noticeable barrier. While a few women spoke of advisors and mentors who were white and/or male, all interviewees mentioned the importance of having mentors who had faced similar challenges and barriers through their identity as women and people of color.

> *"The organizations where I've worked just didn't know how to mentor me, and they just didn't even try. I find it hard to hear them say that they are committed to diversity and inclusion when they aren't willing to work with a woman of color to find a way to provide mentorship that works for me and addresses my reality. Because what they have been doing has kept the systems in place."*
>
> —DIYA, South Asian American educational leader

Kiara, a Black philanthropic leader, shared a moving story of having a woman of color mentor early in her career. She explained that this mentorship gave her confidence, guidance, and support in a way that made sense for her life experiences. Kiara said she had learning and work opportunities that she wouldn't have had without this mentor. She also knew that, sadly, *"this is not the reality for most Black women or other women of color."*

These extra layers and extra efforts add up and deplete us even further. As a survey participant shared, these barriers contribute to the reality that *"there are still so few WOC in positions of power that it's unexpected, and sometimes openly unwelcome to have me in these leadership spaces."*

Despite the extensive evidence of racism in the U.S. and the additional barriers women of color face, some people claim there is such a thing as "reverse racism." Racism is a racialized system of unequal access to power and resources; given this reality, it is impossible to accept the notion of racism against white people in the U.S. since white people, as a group, in the U.S. have disproportionately higher levels of power and resources across all institutions and sectors. So on top of being excluded from traditional models of leadership and mentorship, women of color also face an additional barrier in the assumption that they might have earned a spot in competitive institutions due to preferential treatment for "minorities" (recall Emilia's story earlier).

An example from my own life can help illustrate how this misplaced belief in "reverse racism" finds its way into the lives of women of color. I learned about the doctoral program I applied to from an older white woman who had invited me multiple times to present at workshops for a leadership institute she led. When I mentioned that I was contemplating pursuing a doctorate, she told me about a program that was "really good, but also very competitive and very hard to get into." Then, without missing a beat, she said, "But being Hispanic, you'd probably get in." So just like that, I became aware that I would face some people's assumptions that I got in easily and not for my merit; meanwhile, I had to go through extra layers of gatekeeping and proving my worth to be allowed into this doctorate program.

> *"And we're often the most educated, most degreed people in the room who often have more degrees than our bosses or previous leaders in the same organizations. And so I think it's how it legitimizes you in the world, in the white dominant mainstream world. And I think those of us realize that early on in our careers, we go out and get all the education, and we still face so many misconceptions and then misperceptions that we somehow got in because of affirmative action. And that it's not your accomplishment."*
>
> —ALEJANDRA, Latine philanthropic leader

Although individuals see higher levels of education as a vehicle to opening doors to opportunity, a report from the Building Movement Project finds that "education and training do not provide equity. Women of color with advanced education were more likely than men of color, white men, or white women to work in administrative roles and the least likely to hold senior leadership positions. Women of color also are paid less compared to men of color and white men and more frequently report frustrations with inadequate salaries."[3] Within this reality, women of color invest their resources—money, time, and energy—in extensive education while the systems continue to underestimate, undervalue, and underpay them.

The barriers women of color face in reaching leadership positions are many and multilayered. They are also not equally experienced by all women of color, who have differences in race, immigration status, socio-economic class, disability status, and skin tone. One way you can work to identify these barriers, especially if these barriers have been invisible to you so far, is by conducting an internal audit of the processes and policies at your organization. Ensure grievance processes are in place, and conduct exit interviews for departing employees. Removing barriers from the recruitment, hiring, performance, and exiting processes requires involving human resources and working intentionally and with an applied racial-equity lens internally and externally.

Supremacist Origin Stories

CHAPTER 6

Don't Tell Me about It

(Predominantly white) boards, comfort, and
power: white people's comfort often comes
at the cost of people of color's safety

*Ultimately, privileged people can make their meaning and
impose meaning on the world more than they are required to
accept the meaning-making of others.*

—CYNDI SUAREZ, *The Power Manual*

When the world is built to your specifications, and the default culture
built into institutions and organizational cultures aligns with your experiences and worldview, then anything that challenges your expectation
of comfort is experienced as an attack.[1] The women I spoke to are painfully aware of this and shared many instances of having to keep quiet
and modulate their thoughts, feelings, and worldviews to protect white
comfort in their workplaces. As Jenae Holloway shares, many women of
color feel compelled to carry out the "invisible labor that shields white
people from the extent of our pain."[2] Many workplace experiences come
down to those in power being unable to distinguish between discomfort
and lack of safety. As a Latine nonprofit leader who participated in the
survey explained, echoing sentiments shared by every woman I interviewed, *"The older and wiser I become, I see clearly that my leadership
can make those in power feel threatened."* The following stories provide

examples of cultures valuing and protecting some people's comfort over other people's safety.

Katina: No Accountability in Supremacist Power Structures

When a staff member has a grievance involving the highest levels of staff leadership, that person should be able to confide in a human resources person safely. When that is unavailable, board members should help them navigate and address organizational dysfunctions. Yet I know of multiple situations where identifying any appropriate and safe grievance process is impossible. *If this is the case in your organization, take note.*

In this story, Katina, a woman of color in a junior leadership position hired to do racial equity work, is increasingly concerned about sensitive situations at her office that involve upper management. During her months at the office, Katina has witnessed some bizarre interactions between upper management (especially Kevin, the CEO, and Annie, the CFO, both white) and the rest of the staff and between Kevin and Annie and community leaders. In this situation, Katina is concerned about racialized and gendered interactions and decisions targeting staff and participants of a community leadership program. Because Annie also handles all human resources, there is no one on staff she can turn to. Katina is thinking about approaching the board chair for guidance.

In fact, unknown to Katina, the organization's board chair had heard from more than one (departing) staff member about unhealthy and harmful racial and gender dynamics at the organization. Because of Katina's identity as a woman of color and her experience working to promote equity in nonprofit organizations, Sanjay, the board chair, reached out and asked her to tell him about her experience at the organization. Katina was apprehensive—she had worked at the organization for less than six months and relocated her family for the job. Katina was the sole earner in her household, so she explained to Sanjay the precarious position his request to share potentially damaging insights about the workplace put her in. Sanjay assured Katina he understood: "Why don't you come by my house this weekend? That way, we can talk privately." Katina decided to trust Sanjay, a person of color, and to view this conversation as part of her work to "operationalize racial equity" at her new workplace.

That Sunday, Katina drove to Sanjay's lovely neighborhood and spoke openly but diplomatically, believing that being open about the work culture might bring about needed change to benefit the organization and its community partners. Katina was wringing her hands, choosing her words carefully. Still, she left Sanjay's house feeling heard, seen, and confident that she had spoken up for her coworkers and community partners, who she believed had been mistreated. Katina also felt that because Sanjay is not white, he could relate to some of the concerns she'd shared and that she didn't need to "prove" to Sanjay that racism was real.

Katina remained guarded and anxious the entire week, waiting for something to happen at work. But days turned to weeks turned to months, and nothing came of their conversation. She saw Sanjay at board meetings, coming and going for meetings with Kevin and Annie at the office. To Katina, it felt as if Sanjay pretended that their conversation had never happened. It was confusing and disappointing and certainly didn't help build trust. To continue working at the organization and interacting with Sanjay at meetings, Katina tried to find other ways to address the toxic work culture within the staff structure. But as the dysfunction and abusive behavior toward some staff and troubling interactions with community members continued, Katina decided she needed to speak to Sanjay again, hoping that an update on the situation would move him to action.

Katina texted Sanjay, asking for an opportunity to follow up on their previous conversation. Sanjay responded by setting up a time to speak by phone. Katina called him from her car, never wanting to have these conversations in the office. This time, he did not ask for details but cut the call short by stating that he was about to term out, so he recommended that Katina follow up with the incoming board chair instead. Maybe out of feelings of guilt or to cover his complicity, Sanjay had asked Katina not to mention to the incoming board chair that she had spoken to him about these issues, putting her in a very awkward position and undermining the fact that she had been attempting to address her concerns for some time now.

Katina was disappointed and confused by the conversation. But she had a good relationship with Sue, the incoming chair, so she thought this conversation might be easier and more fruitful than with Sanjay. Katina had developed a personal relationship with Sue, an older white woman, and saw her as a potential mentor. Katina had anticipated a long relationship with Sue, given that they'd also connected personally, as Sue's daughter was engaged to marry a man from Katina's hometown.

Katina emailed Sue from her personal email and asked if they could meet in person at a coffee shop outside of work hours. They had spoken many times before, and going out for coffee was something they'd talked about before. Sue said she'd be delighted to do so and offered some dates in the coming week. "This is a good sign," Katina thought.

She walked in, confident that she could prompt positive workplace changes. Following a hug and friendly greeting, which had put Katina at ease, Sue said, "Now, if this is about Kevin or Annie, I can't talk to you about it."

Taken aback, Katina said, "It's about both of them. But I've already done everything else I could do, including talking to Kevin and Annie directly. Nothing has changed, and I believe I should tell someone on the board about my concerns."

Katina knew it was unfair of Sanjay to ask her not to share that they'd discussed these leadership concerns. However, she still felt that she needed to respect that request—equal parts that she thought herself someone who respected confidentiality and feared that it might result in her losing her job. Not knowing what else to do, Katina looked at Sue and said, "I feel it is my responsibility to inform you, as board chair, of the unhealthy and, I think, the unethical situation at work."

Sue was uncomfortable, and her eyes didn't meet Katina's the way they had in their many prior conversations; instead, Sue shook her head and said she wouldn't engage in a discussion about staff leadership. The board culture of conflict avoidance was coming through, and Katina's heart sank as Sue continued:

"I understand there isn't anyone else for you to go to with these concerns. But I'm sorry, we can't talk about that." *Short pregnant pause.* "Look, I think you're brilliant; you've done great work for the organization, and I will support you and speak to your excellent work if you decide to look for other opportunities. I think you're too far ahead of people in the organization in your thinking, and you might be better off elsewhere. Have you thought about that?"

Sue's words sunk like a heavy rock in Katina's chest. She felt devastated and trapped, like she'd failed herself and her family. As she forced a smile and took sips from her too-hot coffee cup that tasted as bitter as the conversation, she couldn't stop thinking that she'd moved her family to a new place where they had no family or friends for this great job opportunity, where she had been told she would rise through leadership and lead them into meaningful racial justice work.

Along with a growing sense of despair, she felt a personal loss and hurt: Sue was someone Katina thought she had a personal relationship with, someone she respected, someone she had seen as a potential and much-longed-for mentor. Katina felt rejected, devalued, disposable, and silenced.

Katina had been recruited to do racial equity work. Yet it was precisely her concerns about racial and gender dynamics within the organization that prompted Sue to encourage her to look for work elsewhere. With her coffee in hand, she smiled and asked about Sue's family and her daughter's wedding plans. After what felt like an eternity, Katina said she needed to head home for family dinner. She sat in her car feeling betrayed and like she'd been fooled—*how did she not know better by now?* Why did she think she could trust Sue? Why did she think this organization would be different from others where she'd been brought in to add diversity and *operationalize* racial equity but been blocked when she tried to bring actual change? What caused Sue, a seasoned professional with extensive board experience, to shrug off her responsibility to at least hear staff concerns about the organization's leadership?

In the coming weeks, Katina faced the fact that staying would mean being silenced or having to continue to work for change without the support of the board or staff leadership. With support from her family, Katina made the difficult decision to follow Sue's backhanded advice and start looking for other jobs. The organization where Katina worked was well-known in a small community. Katina knew that part of its dysfunction manifested in staff leadership bad-mouthing staff who didn't conform to the dominant culture. She and her family would need to move again to find a job. This decision would not be without personal cost—Katina would be moving her kids again to a new school and community, and the not-insignificant financial cost of such a move.

After Katina left the organization, she wondered how these board leaders justified that she was not the first to leave due to toxic organizational culture, and that every staff member who'd left was a woman, and half were women of color. Sue never spoke to Katina again. Sanjay emailed Katina at her personal email months after she left to congratulate her but never mentioned anything about their conversations. To this day, Katina feels sick and dizzy when she sees that organization getting recognized and written up for its excellent racial equity work and support of the community.

Following, Rosario's story painfully illustrates how boards can too easily abuse their power and use it to control and punish leaders who challenge the status quo. Rosario is the executive director of an organization serving the Latinx community.

> *"I had a situation with very abusive board members, and they asked me to do things that weren't right. I spoke up when they asked me to do something that wasn't right, and because I dared to contradict them, they were determined to get me fired.*

For example, I was a one-person show, and they wanted all these reports. I said that my priority had to be attending to clients in person first, so the reports had to come second after our clients. I told the board members I was sorry but would not answer the phone when they called if I was with a client and that the report was not more important than the people we supported. And the board chair said to me, yelling, 'I am your boss, and you don't know who you are talking to.'

I told her, 'You don't know who you're talking to either; I am this organization's executive director and its founder, so you don't yell at me.' Then she started crying and talking to the other white ladies on the board, who also felt threatened by the fact that I didn't let them mistreat me. And this included white Latinas on the board, too.

They were mad and decided to demote me and decrease my salary. They started to say things about me to others [outside the organization], and eventually, one of them wrote a letter to the state and accused me of embezzling. As a result, I had to spend a year with an audit by the state because of a grant we received from the state.

And a very funny thing happened due to the audit: the state realized that they were paying us less than the worth of the work, and they could have gotten in trouble. So the state doubled the amount of funds, renewed their grant to us for two more years, and gave us more money, and, to this day, we still receive a grant from them. And, they found no wrongdoing on my part at all."

Threats to the comfort of the powerful can elicit abusive behavior from individuals one might never suspect from engaging in gaslighting, disinformation, or harm. People who are used to power (whether they are aware of this or not) feel entitled to comfort, to being the center of attention, to being in the presumed gaze of desired objects, and to having their perspectives and skills valued and recognized.

Eliana: The Unexamined Board

Two years into her tenure, Eliana, a CEO at a foundation, had gone through multiple consultants hired to help address board tensions and dysfunction. Nothing about board or staff tensions or challenges had been mentioned during the interview process. Yet shortly after starting the job, Eliana became aware that problems were rampant among staff and board.

Eliana and her team experienced the board as micromanaging and paternalistic. The board frequently ignored or sidelined work that staff had done, made unplanned demands of Eliana's and other staff's time and organizational resources, and made operational decisions without including Eliana. Eliana shared with the board chair that staff didn't feel trusted by the board, partly because of how board members spoke to and treated staff at board meetings. To her surprise, George, the board chair, was furious at hearing this and told Eliana not to use the term *trust*: "No, I do trust you. I feel like I trust you and the staff, so that's just not true. When you say I don't trust you, I am so upset that I don't want to talk anymore. You're not helping the situation by saying things like that."

Taken aback by his anger, she did her best to model calm through her voice and careful choice of words: "George, I understand that it is not your intention to make me or the staff feel like we are not trusted. But I am sharing my experience with you, as you have repeatedly asked me to do. I am not questioning your intention; I am sharing the impact of board actions and words on me and the rest of the staff. There is a power dynamic between board and staff that is creating a lot of stress and a lot of hurt." George was undeterred and insisted that Eliana's pushing back was the problem. A few weeks later, George told Eliana that he was tired of the tensions between her (and other staff) and some board members and that Eliana needed to "have it out," especially with board member Brianne.

"That's not my style; I will not have it out with anyone. And I've had a few one-on-one conversations with Brianne, which are always fine. The problem is not interpersonal; it is about individual board members taking independent action without board approval or knowledge and without involving or informing me as ED. It comes down to the same issue we've discussed for the past couple of years: the board is one entity, and individual board members shouldn't direct staff to do work like Brianne repeatedly does."

George was determined to solve Eliana's problem. "You just need to sit down with Brianne again and have it out. Get mad at each other and figure it out."

For months, these frustrating conversations with George continued. He treated Eliana like his assistant, asking her to register him for events and made statements and decisions outside good governance. A few board members were aware of this and disagreed with his behavior, but to not ruffle feathers, no one confronted him directly. Eliana was at a breaking point, so she decided to speak frankly to George. Sitting in her home office facing George on the Zoom screen, Eliana felt flustered and unnerved. She squeezed her hands tightly and practiced slow breathing to calm her heartbeat, aware that the person on the screen (who had referred to her as CEO of the staff, not the whole organization) making her job (and increasingly her life) miserable could fire her. She spoke in an unnaturally calm tone, picking her words intentionally and almost unemotionally, refuting yet another suggestion that she have it out with Brianne:

"George, I would like to ask you to put yourself in my shoes for a moment and think about the position that challenging a board member in that way would put me in. Ultimately, the board can fire me, and Brianne has a lot of power within the board. So when you suggest I should have it out with her, you ask me to risk my family's livelihood. If I lost this job, I wouldn't be able to pay for my child's college, and soon after, I would be unable to cover my mortgage and other expenses. This is not an option for me, given that I do not have a contract or severance package."

Part of what fueled Eliana's determination to speak to George was that she had asked the board for a severance package over a year ago. The board had repeatedly delayed its decision on the severance policy.

Eliana couldn't help but notice that some board members treated her increasingly worse and seemed to be holding the severance policy out as a reminder of their power over her.

George was quiet for the first time in their conversation. When he finally spoke, he said, "Hmmm. I guess it never occurred to me that you wouldn't be able to quit if you were unhappy. I've made sure I have enough money so that if I don't like something, I can walk away." George then talked about how he had been so successful in his business. Eliana was deflated at the end of the unnecessarily long conversation. Despite the many equity trainings to the board, her board chair had not considered her situation in the ongoing tensions with the board. More than ever, she felt that she couldn't count on the support or guidance of the board.

Eliana shared that, over the following months, a few board members continued to reprimand her for disagreeing with board members or asking questions about opaque board processes, with George going so far as to write up a letter of complaints against her and forcing her to meet with a few board members to answer, point by point, the accusations on the letter. Eventually, the rest of the board stepped in and brought these personal attacks to an end, having found all allegations to be, at best, misrepresentations. Eliana rode out the dysfunction out of necessity until new board members were recruited. New board members were perplexed and concerned about the dynamics between the board, Eliana, and staff. Thankfully, Eliana saw new board members (recruited through an open-call process) speak up and challenge the abusive dynamics. As board leadership changed, Eliana observed the vast difference values-driven membership and governance policies can make for organizational culture.

WHAT THIS EXPERIENCE CAN TEACH US

In varied and mundane ways, the comfort of people with structural power can cause harm to women of color. Power in organizations needs to be decentralized to prevent and mitigate such harm, and alternative reporting processes need to account for situations when people in positions of ultimate power are the ones causing harm. Eliana and Katina had nowhere to go for guidance and support. There was no functional grievance process, no mediation, and no way for them to report the misbehaviors. Their boards were mired in dysfunction and preoccupied with their internal tensions and individual power. In Eliana's case, the board chair was blind to his privilege and had limited governance experience. In Katina's case, the board chair had extensive experience but chose her comfort over her responsibility to ensure that the organization was true to its values.

In other words, shrugging responsibility because it makes you uncomfortable is white privilege. Choosing not to see the harm because it doesn't affect you is white privilege (or upholding white privilege if you are a person of color, as in the situations with George and Sanjay). Ignoring repeated reports of harm to staff and community (particularly when it is women and staff of color who are reporting harm and leaving) while witnessing significant staff turnover at the organization where you are a board member makes you complicit to the harm. Too often, board members fail to address institutional and systemic issues in favor of interpersonal relationship-building—*let's go for dinner and drinks, a board retreat somewhere beautiful, smile and be pleasant.* They invest in the interpersonal and ignore the structural, while silencing any concerns about the board or organizational culture. The discomfort of witnessing or being complicit in injustice or abuse is just too much for too many people.

We could do a deep dive into what makes boards more effective, but the reality is that boards are outdated constructs that were not created to advance equity, justice, or community. We don't need to educate or reform boards—*we must completely reimagine governance.* There is no place for supremacist structures in liberated spaces. Until we have new nonprofit governance models, a great starting place is "Decolonizing Your Board" by Natalie A. Walrond. Walrond describes a decolonized board as "founded on values of mutual respect, honesty, integrity, and transparency in communication between the nonprofit's board and leadership."[3] She says that boards should "create the conditions that the leadership team needs to operate the nonprofit with integrity, agility, and innovation." She offers nine liberatory strategies to guide boards in the ongoing work of decolonization:

1. Be part of the solution

2. Lead with abundance

3. Share the work

4. Engage productively in the process

5. Let the mission set the agenda

6. Upend traditional power dynamics

7. Share your networks

8. Respect the leadership team

9. Value well-being[4]

Of importance, boards have historically been, and remain, predominantly white and nonrepresentative of the communities their organizations serve and represent. In "Nonprofit Boards Efforts to Diversify,"[5] Aracely Muñoz addresses nonprofit boards' slow diversification (with some improvements in gender and age diversity in the past few years) and the importance of lived experience, noting its pronounced absence in most nonprofit boards.

Still, Muñoz cites a 2021 BoardSource study of nonprofit boards that "found that 22 percent identified as either African American, Asian, Hispanic, Native American, biracial or multiracial, or other."[6] While an improvement from 16 percent in 2017, United States Census data in 2020 show that "42 percent of the country's population identifies with one or more of these racial and ethnic categories, indicating a clear underrepresentation of these groups on nonprofit boards."[7] Boards also have disproportionately low representation of people with one or more disabilities. This lack of representation matters because "the people an organization selects to join its board shape how that organization will grow and serve its communities."[8]

In the U.S., the origins of boards came with colonizer settlers in New England. Boards were conceived and continue to hold "powerful informal norms of deference" and other underlying assumptions of elitism.[9] Boards often operate through private personal networks, emphasizing relationships as the currency for influence. Relationships, like power, are not innately good or bad, so just emphasizing relationships does not signal equity or justice. It is also important to note that nonprofit boards in the U.S. act, in many ways, as "shadow state" actors due to the late-twentieth-century shift away from government responsibility and provision for essential services of our populations and toward the privatized provision of community services. In the U.S., populations rely more on nonprofit organizations than their communities or government, emphasizing individualistic (as opposed to collectivist) views, values, and approaches. Nonprofit boards seldom represent the interests of communities, with a majority of nonprofit board members believing they are ultimately accountable to themselves only or to no one at all, as noted by Judith Millesen in the 2019 article "Who 'Owns' Your Nonprofit?"[10] For a humorous and no less accurate perspective on why boards bring out toxic behavior in otherwise "good" people, see Vu Le's piece "Why Do So Many Nice People Become Assholes When They Join a Board?"[11]

Nonprofit and foundation staff frequently cite boards as a barrier to change and a significant consumer of staff (and therefore, organizational) resources; step into any conference, webinar, or after-hours work event, and boards are a primary source of venting and frustration. Yet despite considering them a universally acknowledged design flaw in the nonprofit world, we generally replicate these same structures over and over, repeating dysfunction in the places where we spend disproportionate amounts of our lives. This is not an indictment of individual board members or even individual boards; it is a recognition that the concept and structure of boards as governance are in many ways intrinsically antithetical to the values and missions of many of the organizations that these boards are working to advance. Boards are not only generally nonrepresentative of the communities they serve; they are, in essence, a structure in which individuals who periodically drop into the work of an organization determine its direction and strategies while demanding deference from those carrying the daily work. This makes no sense!

Let me be clear: Every woman of color I interviewed who worked with a board mentioned boards as a source of mistreatment. This seems especially true for women of color leaders who challenge the status quo of power dynamics and work to change organizational culture. Within a justice framework, those closest to the issues being worked on should have the strongest voices, which is seldom the case in nonprofits or foundations. Our structures must manifest our claimed values to change our cultures.

But regardless of the limitations of current governance constructs, if fear, comfort, or self-interest get in the way of responsibilities, you morally forfeit the right to the power bestowed upon you by your membership on the board. When you act for yourself at the expense of the collective, you are part of the problem. Your comfort should never trump the safety of other people, particularly those who have significantly less positional power and stand to lose resources, opportunities, or dignity by safeguarding your status.

The stories shared in this section also highlight what Brené Brown calls a *shame culture* at work, where the culture "mandates that it is more important to protect the reputation of that system and those in power than it is to protect the basic human dignity of individuals or communities."[12] This description of what Brown calls a "shame infestation" reads as if it was written about Katina's, Eliana's, and Rosario's experiences.

In the situation with Katina, we have to make visible the personal cost to her and her family: from the disappointment that individuals she thought she had a relationship with repeatedly ignored reports of harm to staff, to being put in a situation where she either had to compromise her ethical standards or leave her family's only source of income (and health insurance), to her family having to relocate again, to the harm and trauma of witnessing her workplace harm its staff and community members, and the invisible harm to Katina's confidence and psychic well-being. In my career, I have repeatedly experienced how loyalty to systems of power and privilege (including elite or exclusive circles, such as boards) often supersedes interpersonal relationships and service to a mission or set of values. Privilege is *that* compelling.

Suppose you are in a position of responsibility and authority at a place with high turnover, especially if those leaving are mostly women, people of color, LGBTQIA, or persons with disabilities. You should consider it an invitation to look closer. Looking closer may include listening to staff members who express concerns or incidents of harm. In Rosario's story, other board members should have been aware of the dynamics between the executive director and their peers on the board and intervened. While no one denies that it is uncomfortable to disagree with or confront your fellow board members, your ability to do so when necessary is integral to your governance obligation. Conflict avoidance is the downfall of effective governance.

Working in a values-based or -driven way is not easy, and it will inevitably bring conflict. Conflict, when handled with care and respect, can be part of meaningful change. Because all members of an organization share responsibility for the culture of the organization, there is no room for shrugging responsibility just because it is uncomfortable. Avoiding conflict in the face of reported harm is never an appropriate way to support an organization's mission.

Ask yourself: Where can an organizational leader go when the board or board chair is a primary source of harm and dysfunction? What protections does your organization offer your leadership and the rest of the staff? What compensation and severance package considerations are in place for leaders who don't draw on generational wealth, trusts, or personal wealth? For leaders who are sole earners for their families? For leaders who relocate for a job and lack a safety net in the community? What vehicles for mediation exist within the organization if the trouble is with leadership? Has your human resources department (or staff) had training in racial equity? Do you have a whistleblower policy?

CHAPTER 7

White Supremacy Is the Air We All Breathe

The scarcity of seats at the table of power, combined with internalized oppression and white supremacy, can lead women of color to uphold harmful power structures at the expense of other women of color

It's only more recently that we understand how much facing racial bias and discrimination at work takes a mental health toll, so it's critical for women of color to prioritize their well-being. Develop coping strategies, find a support network, and make an exit strategy. Most importantly, understand that you're not to blame for systemic workplace bias.

—RUCHIKA TULSHYAN, "The Psychological Toll of Being the Only Woman of Color at Work," *Harvard Business Review*

During every interview for this book, there was a moment when the woman I was talking to told me a story about another person of color (most often another woman of color) enforcing and protecting the power structure of white supremacy at the expense of other people of color. This is an important reminder that "anyone can use patterns of domination, regardless of race, class, gender, or other difference."[1] Or as an Asian

American survey participant put it, *"Sometimes instead of being supportive, WOC are antagonistic and toxic in relating to / working with other WOC. It is a sad reality that I have frequently experienced."*

There is a particular heaviness to the sadness that this dynamic brings; it signals the death of solidarity in the relationship with that person and creates a type of gaslighting that is difficult to shake. Although I have personally experienced this multiple times, I first read about this dynamic within workplaces in the book *Decolonizing Wealth*.[2] In its description of "House Slaves," "Field Hands," and "Overseers," it felt like a weight lifted from me to know that others recognized this as a very real dynamic in our workplaces. *White supremacy is in the air we all breathe.*

I, and other women of color leaders I have spoken to, have seen this show up in different ways. A few of the women I interviewed raised this dynamic as a tough one to talk about and asked me to please include it in this book to address it more openly and carefully. As an Indigenous nonprofit leader shared in the survey, *"The tendency is to look at power as dominance and the need to join the patriarchal leadership structure by cutting down other women. Instead, we should look for ways to create a living expression of sisterhood."*

One pervasive way this shows up is by adopting a scarcity mindset: a belief that having more than one or two people of color in positions of influence is not realistic or sustainable. The you-or-me, kill-or-be-killed mentality pits women of color against other women of color; it is doing the oppressor's work while reaching for personal gain or protection. I've personally witnessed an immigrant community leader speak against trusting immigrants, saying that *they* should learn the value of working hard and earning their place at the table; I've heard a Black leader say that we can't trust people just because they're Black—*and imply that's what racial justice means*—and, in so doing, advocating against any prioritization of Black applicants to a leadership program that was disproportionately overrepresented with white leaders. These instances are deeply sad, in part, because most women I spoke to recognized this dynamic as a maladaptive survival mechanism.

Jennifer Magley speaks to the uniquely painful experience of a woman of color being undermined or attacked by another woman of color. In her article "How Toxic Work Culture Breeds Unnecessary Competition between Black Employees,"[3] Magley shares about her experience as a Black woman being undermined at work by another Black professional whom she had seen as a potential mentor. Toxic workplace culture and women of color so often being the "only" at their workplace contribute to this competition, Magley says. She proposes intentional community-building and trust-building as the antidote.

In the book *Dismantling Institutional Whiteness*, Cristina Alcalde (my sister!) and Mangala Subramaniam share the following about the experience of being the only or the first:

> There is additional labor and risk attached to being the "first." Fulfilling the responsibilities involves interfacing with a gendered and racialized face of university administration and specifically the emotional labor that becomes an integral part of the lives of women of color whose performance is closely monitored and critiqued as we are simultaneously made invisible and hypervisible, depending on the circumstances. Dismantling structures of oppression implies a significant investment of emotional labor in efforts to disrupt the status quo.[4]

As Soledad, a Latine philanthropic leader, shared, *"It's been really interesting for me to watch how well trained, how engrained it [white supremacy] is in our thought process and approaches. And how painful it is when another woman of color upholds white patriarchal supremacist values and systems over us. And throwing us under the bus because we're seen as a threat to the power within conformity versus the power we're trying to bring, which is resistance.*

"And I think that what is creating a lot of the infighting right now among BIPOC people is that some want to conform and believe that they've gotten to where they've gotten because they have conformed, and some are fighting and trying to make things different. And that tension, I think, is our undoing."

Workplaces that create *Hunger Games* cultures put people in survival mode, which leads them to act in ways that don't necessarily align with their values. Many years ago, a Black woman who had been consulting for the organization where I worked (we were experiencing significant workplace harm) called me and apologized to me. When I asked what she was apologizing for, she stated that for the first few months of her engagement with our organization, she had inadvertently adopted the views and attitudes of those with most positional power without questioning their views, and in doing so, had silenced, undermined, and harmed me (and others). She acknowledged that she had been successful in her career by adopting certain leadership (and dominance) approaches that worked well in white-dominant spaces, and they had become all too easy to call upon and use. I was deeply moved by this courageous and vulnerable self-awareness and the fortitude to say it directly to me. I was equally deeply saddened and hurt when she continued the behavior she had apologized for and further contributed to the toxic behavior of certain individuals with positional power. Most disturbingly, the people responsible for the harmful behavior (who were individuals of color as well) accused others in the organization of racism, blatantly undermining the collective work for our shared liberation. These few individuals had confused anti-racism work and liberation with self-promotion and individual power gains. This was not the first or only, and likely will not be the last, experience I've had with a woman of color treating other women of color as direct competition for scarce resources or opportunities.

These stories remind us that we cannot essentialize justice work—we cannot simply assume that one's identity will determine our approach to white supremacy. This phenomenon of women of color undermining other women of color emphasizes the importance of not confusing diversity or representation for justice or equity. Trauma is complex, cannibalizing what it must to survive, disguising itself in multiple forms, and sometimes adopting the very source of our injury as our armor. A supremacist society with Black and Brown people in charge is still supremacist and cannot supplant liberation or engender healing.

WHAT THIS EXPERIENCE CAN TEACH US

We must understand that white supremacy and patriarchy are the air we breathe and the default setting of our institutions and institutional cultures. *None* of us is naturally immune to it. We must not essentialize people in a way that implicates white people as oppressors and Black and Brown people as champions of liberation or, worse, natural victims. We must also not conflate equity, which works at the systems and structural levels, with personal position and power, which focus on individual gain.

For those who identify as a person of color, pay attention to the stories you tell yourself about other people of color in your professional sphere. Listen to how you mentally distinguish yourself from individuals from (other) communities of color, and how class, gender, ethnicity, immigration status, disability, and skin color play into your mental models. For those identifying as white, please pay attention to white guilt and discomfort. I, and the women I have spoken to, all talked about situations in which a white person in a position of power was overwhelmed and confused by being told different perspectives by different people of color, to the point that the white person was paralyzed. Educate yourself by reading about racial capitalism, and understand the slippery slope of objectifying people who belong to populations that are not considered white in the U.S. Think about the incentives and systems in place that may give the implicit (or explicit) message that there is only room for one (or any limited number) of people of color in positions of influence or power.

> *"We have internalized this idea of scarcity on some level and are competing for resources. That is partially why some women of color feel like they must run over other women of color."*
>
> —SHANTI, Asian American nonprofit leader

While the theme didn't come up as much in the interviews, we cannot explore the intersection of race and gender without naming colorism, or skin tone bias. Colorism has genuine impacts and consequences on Black women in the U.S., as well as on Latines and other women of color in the U.S.[5] A few of the women I interviewed named colorism as a complicated dynamic to prove or talk about, which adds further layers of complexity to the intersectional experiences of women of color. As Ruchika Tulshyan states in her article "How Colorism Affects Women at Work," colorism "is an insidious form of bias that impacts women with darker skin tones across ethnicities and races . . . One of the more insidious aspects of colorism is that it's tough to prove, and there's often no recourse for those who experience it."[6] One concrete recommendation in the article is to ensure that colorism is included in your organization's DEI efforts and explicitly named in discrimination policies. Soledad, a Latine philanthropic leader, named colorism as an important and challenging aspect of discrimination to engage with. She reflected on the ways that white supremacy creates hierarchies of oppression, and how communities of color, in this case Latine and Latin American cultures, enforce white supremacy by practicing anti-Blackness and colorism within communities of color, saying, *"I also think that it's about shades of color."* I recommend reading Sarah Webb for more about colorism.[7]

Understand that divide and conquer has been an effective and common tactic in the U.S. since colonial times, and all who have been raised in this culture have it implanted in our subconscious so that it feels natural and generally invisible. This fact is indeed one of the truest manifestations of the power of white supremacy culture. As Suarez states in *The Power Manual*, "This is the ultimate power, for it is the power to shape desire, such that one cannot help but internalize dominant values and beliefs, and support institutional procedures that favor the dominant."[8]

CHAPTER 8

Divide and Conquer

White supremacy uses paternalism, condescension, gaslighting, and control to ward off threats to its existence—as does an abusive partner in an intimate relationship

History is full of examples of divide and conquer, a favored age-old strategy of colonialism.[1] Divide and conquer is a story of the powerful preventing the systematically exploited and oppressed from seeing their shared fate and joining forces; divide and conquer pits groups against each other to distract and redirect energy away from those who wield power, thereby preventing solidarity and collective power *with*. This historical tactic at the root of white supremacy is employed in workplaces. One particularly strange situation that illustrates this dynamic involves Elisa.

Elisa: The Strange Ways White Supremacy Enforces Compliance

Elisa was a relatively new staff member hired to work on racial equity. She was one of a few staff members of color. Since joining the organization, and as part of what Elisa saw as her role, she had asked several questions about organizational structure and culture—like who participated in what meetings, who contributed to developing job descriptions, meeting agendas, work plans and timelines, and who had access to developing or even seeing the program budget, among others—that made staff leadership uncomfortable and defensive. This defensiveness at Elisa's inquiries took a strange turn when (white) senior management told some staff members (all people of color) that it was inappropriate to spend work time socializing, even though this same (white) senior manager frequently spent long amounts of time socializing and joking with two of the same staff (not at the same time, though).

Lindy, a timid white staff member, had initially caught Elisa's attention. In the first few weeks at work, Elisa learned that some of the staff thought Lindy was being treated badly by senior management, raising their voice at her, demanding work after-hours, and gaslighting when Lindy voiced concerns or complaints. Over the past couple of weeks, Lindy had been getting help from Elisa on a challenging, time-sensitive project.

Lindy had confided in Elisa. "I'm so stressed about this project and the timeline. I've never done something like this, and I don't know if I can do it by the deadline. I'm doing this alone, and I need help."

Elisa could tell Lindy was anxious about this project and knew she had been working late a lot. Knowing that the senior manager, Joan, had set a bafflingly unrealistic timeline for completion without consulting Lindy, Elisa asked, "Have you talked to Joan about this? Do you know why she set the timeline so short? I mean, I'm happy to help you however I can. I helped a former coworker on a similar project a few years ago—I'm not sure I would be a lot of help, but I'm happy to offer support and help think through questions that come up if you like." Elisa knew her support was likely emotional as it was technical, and she could tell that Lindy needed both.

"Yes, I would appreciate that. I can't get a hold of the rep to ask for guidance on how to set up parts of the new database, and it would help to have you help me figure out some of the programmatic pieces since I am not as familiar with those." Lindy seemed relieved, and the two returned to Lindy's office to review the work.

A few days into Elisa and Lindy working together for a few hours a day on the project, Joan came to Lindy's office in the morning and closed the door. Later that day, Elisa went into Lindy's office to ask how it was going.

"I can't talk to you about it; I'll get in trouble," Lindy said nervously, without making eye contact. "Maybe don't come to my office again today."

Elisa was super confused but thought Lindy was stressed and needed a quiet day in her office. Elisa had a lot of work to catch up on, so she didn't see Lindy until the end of the day. At the end of the day, when most others had gone home, Lindy went to Elisa's office and tearfully confided:

"I'm so sorry; she told me I couldn't have you help me on the project anymore. She wouldn't tell me why, but she told me that I couldn't ask you for help and that I shouldn't have you come into my office to work on the project with me anymore." Elisa didn't understand but let the visibly upset Lindy continue: "I still need your help. Can you help me now that she's gone for the day? Can I text you when I have questions? There's no way I can finish this by the deadline by myself."

Elisa opened her mouth to speak, still trying to understand what Lindy was saying to her, but Lindy interrupted: "Elisa, please don't say anything to her. Don't tell her I told you about this or that I am asking for help."

Elisa assured Lindy she wouldn't tell Joan and that they would figure out a way for her to support Lindy without Joan knowing about it.

This bizarre behavior made Elisa feel dumbfounded and indignant about how she and Lindy were being treated. She wanted to raise this issue at a staff meeting. Still, the reality was that Lindy would have felt the consequences, so she felt compelled to play into the weird dynamic by meeting with Lindy when no one else was around, responding to questions by text, and other surreptitious encounters so that she could do what organizations should encourage and support: collective work for collective aims.

Behavior like this is not usually an isolated incident but is often a symptom of a dysfunctional and controlling organizational culture. This whole episode took place a few months into what can only be described as an effort to disenfranchise Elisa from her coworkers and exclude her from important meetings. For example, two other staff members were told they were spending too much time chatting with Elisa and warned they should limit such socializing. Then, as part of office shifts, Elisa's office was relocated, without consultation, to the end of a hallway, the furthest possible point from her coworkers and next to another organization's offices. Elisa noticed some meetings on her calendar were removed, and she assumed they were canceled. Instead, she was shocked to walk past the conference room glass door and see her boss and a few peers from other organizations whom she'd been talking with for months about potential collaboration on racial equity work meeting together without her.

Around this time, the organization hired a consultant who was told by the CEO of the organization that there was a lot of *gossiping* going on at the organization. The concerns that staff had expressed about work culture, including racist interactions and things such as telling staff not to work with other staff, were interpreted by the organization's leadership as *gossip*. Elisa observed that anything that challenged the status quo and the correctness of the white-savior leadership was labeled gossip and called unprofessional. (See Monique Judge's piece on professionalism as a racist construct.[2])

Toward the end of Elisa's time at this workplace, she began to see the frightening parallels between the work culture there and the dynamics of abusive intimate relationships, including controlling who you are allowed to spend time with, gaslighting, and mocking concerns—as well as providing raises and promotions (golden handcuffs[3]) when long-serving staff became unhappy and started to push back on leadership.

Half the staff left within two years because of the organization's toxic culture. No consequences ever came to CEO Eric or manager Joan. Some of the leaders involved in this story continue to work as leaders in what might be called social justice and equity in nonprofit/philanthropic ecosystems.

WHAT THIS EXPERIENCE CAN TEACH US

Supremacist cultures and systems are abusive, with patterns and strategies similar to domestic violence perpetrators. A few of the women I interviewed described the culture at some places they'd worked in terms that mirror how we describe intimate partner violence. Both workplaces with supremacist cultures and intimate partner violence relationships are upheld by power and control; they use fear, intimidation, and various forms of violence to enforce the control and power structure. They use multiple strategies to maintain the status quo, and do a highly effective job of controlling or eliminating people who attempt to disrupt the power dynamic or question the status quo–reinforcing culture.

Employees who ask questions about the rationale or purpose of certain practices or who advocate for peers or community partners are cast as disloyal and dangerous. When multiple individuals show such "disloyal" tendencies, they must be kept apart and undermined to hollow their potential power of solidarity and collective change (*divide and conquer in colonizing practices, isolate and undermine in intimate partner violence*).

These dynamics sometimes coexist with the peculiar tendency of some workplaces to refer to themselves as being "like family." As David Burkus says in "Why a Company Is Not a Family—and How Companies Can Bond with Their Employees Instead," not only does this framing blur the lines between work and personal life by demanding loyalty and blind trust, but it also makes it easier for employers to exploit employees' time and violate their boundaries.[4] Like abusive families, these organizations control relationships among coworkers while policing and micromanaging behaviors and expression of perspectives among staff. They label anyone who leaves or who questions anything in the organization in terms of loyalty and betrayal. These workplaces practice fear and control in place of trust and care for the people within and outside the organization.

Sometimes it is difficult to see controlling behavior when it is interspersed with symptoms of golden handcuffs. Especially in philanthropy, it can be difficult to choose to leave a well-paying job with generous benefits, knowing that too many nonprofit jobs will not be as well paid and may not have necessary benefits such as paid time off—and health insurance (a cruel reality in a nation where health care is fully commodified and tied to employment, with few exceptions). I have seen places where raises, promotions, and other benefits were used strategically to quell any stirring concerns or complaints about organizational culture. Leaving the economic security of a philanthropic (or well-paid nonprofit or academic) job can be challenging, even in the face of dysfunction, abuse, and personal harm.

CHAPTER 9

Having the Last Word

Supremacist cultures must have the final word, and they will be punitive and vengeful to remind you of "your place"

One of the most egregious, petty, and concretely harmful situations I'll share in this book is about Moira, a woman of color who shared a story about when she was preparing to leave a job that had become harmful to her health and well-being.

Moira: The Punitive Nature of White Supremacy

Moira loved her work but recognized the broader context of her workplace as deeply dysfunctional. For example, Moira had found out from a colleague at another organization that Moira's boss had been telling leaders of partner organizations things that were untrue about Moira, covering his mistakes by telling them that Moira had ignored his directions: "You know, she just does whatever she wants, and I don't even know about it. I had no idea about the changes she made to the meeting. I am just as shocked as you are."

At one point, Moira had a conversation with Daniel, a Black community leader who asked to meet with her away from her office to share a story about Moira's boss, Joe, and his treatment of the community leader. Joe, a white man who is the CEO of a foundation, coerced Daniel into not accepting a portion of a leadership program stipend because Daniel had missed a session in order to meet with another funder about a community project that needed more funding.

Moira was aware that white community leaders in the same program had missed a session (or more) with no monetary impact, and she was disturbed by this racialized and inequitable use of power. Because of the power inequities between funders and community members, Daniel asked Moira not to share this story at her organization—he just needed someone to know about it. And he wanted her to be aware of these dynamics and pay attention if it happened again.

While Moira was having these troubling conversations, she was also excluded from key decision-making meetings. Joe would proclaim at board meetings, in front of Moira, that he had worked with Moira on a specific proposal while she sat there knowing that she had been excluded from all conversations about the topic—all she could do was sit there dumbfounded by the blatant lie. At the same time, presentations at board meetings excluded the work that Moira was leading.

Moira stayed at this job for two years, which is how long it took her to fully realize that senior management had certain patterns of behavior that directly undermined the organization's mission. Once she understood that she was being blocked from influencing change and that her mental and physical health were being affected by dysfunction and aggression, she began to take vacation days to interview for other jobs, and soon she received multiple offers.

After deciding on her next steps, she set up a meeting with the CEO, Joe, to discuss her departure and give him a formal letter of resignation with thirty days' notice, so she could wrap up work and transition it to other staff as needed. She decided, for her mental health, that she would not try to talk with Joe about why she was leaving, given that Joe was a significant contributor to the unhealthy work culture. At the meeting, Joe responded to Moira's resignation without surprise and produced a few pleasant words. "Moira, congratulations, and I am not surprised at all. You are brilliant, and I have no doubt you are going to do great things. I appreciate the thirty days' notice, and I know how much you care about the work you've been doing. This is so exciting."

Relieved, Moira explained that she'd need to use COBRA (Consolidated Omnibus Budget Reconciliation Act) since she wanted to take a couple of weeks off in between jobs. Joe assured Moira that they would keep her and her family on the organization's health insurance until the new job insurance kicked in, so that COBRA (which is very expensive) would not be necessary. "Just talk to Jenny about this, but it won't be a problem. Jenny will get the paperwork for you, and just let us know if you need anything from us." Despite the weird dynamics at work, Moira thought that the resignation seemed to go without drama. She was starting to feel a release of the anxiety and existential dread that had greeted her every morning for nearly two years.

Moira followed up with Jenny and shared a copy of the resignation letter. They agreed to meet the following day to lay out how to create a transition plan for Moira's work and portfolio of grantees to other staff and to start thinking about a job search to fill the vacancy.

The next day, Jenny approached Moira. "I am sure you must have so much to do to prepare for the new job, and you want some downtime, so why don't you plan on wrapping things up in two weeks instead of thirty days? I think that'll work better for everyone."

Surprised, Moira responded, "I appreciate the concern, but I have much to transition to other staff." Sensing the pressure to get her transition plan in place ASAP, she spent the next day working late, creating a list of items she was responsible for, and identifying the next steps to transfer each item to other staff. Moira met with Jenny to run some ideas by her: as part of the transition plan, Moira agreed not to tell staff she was leaving until Joe told the board. This happened within a day, so Moira was able to tell each of her coworkers and touch base on some ideas for transitioning grantees and other work to some of them. Jenny and Moira also agreed that they wouldn't mention anything to the new grantees until they determined who would be their new contact. Moira continued to work on the transition plan, set up communications with anyone who needed to be in the loop, and wrote a few pro forma emails, copying Jenny, to ensure that key organizational contacts had Jenny's name and contact information for future communication.

Three days after Moira submitted her resignation, Jenny, the manager who often carried out Joe's decisions (Joe never spoke to Moira again after the resignation meeting), came into Moira's office: "Hi there, this is for you." Jenny handed Moira a long, typed document on letterhead. Assuming it was an HR formality, Moira took the letter smiling and sat down to read it while Jenny stood at the doorway. It was a letter terminating Moira's employment, *effective immediately.*

Maybe in response to Moira's shocked expression, Jenny spoke: "You violated our agreement. You weren't supposed to tell anyone outside the organization that you were leaving. As you have violated our agreement, your employment has been terminated as of today."

Moira was beyond floored. She looked at Jenny in disbelief and said, "I don't understand. I have done everything we talked about. I have not told the new grantees about my departure, as we haven't decided who will take over that part of my work. I never said I wouldn't tell *anyone* about my leaving; it would be impossible to set things up to transition from me to other staff without letting some people know. I emailed former grantees to let them know about my departure and express my appreciation for the time I've spent with them since we'd worked so closely for the past eighteen months. I copied you on that email, and I copied our grants manager; some of the former grantees have extensions for their final reports, so they need to know who to submit those to, and I won't be here. I am really confused because, in my email, I told them what you and I agreed on regarding submitting the reports. And you're copied on all my communications about my departure."

Jenny stood in the doorway, "We're not going to discuss this. It's done. You violated the agreement, and you should pack your things up and leave."

"I'm genuinely confused," Moira continued, "I just don't understand. My email is a standard, polite one, not unlike other communications I've seen that people send when they transition out of a job. I copied the two people at the office, including you, who would need to be in touch with these former grantees. Why would I copy you if I was violating an agreement we made? That doesn't even make sense. What did Joe say about this?"

Jenny shook her head, "The decision is made. Joe and I have already talked about this. It's done." Jenny walked away, leaving Moira in shock.

Moira sat at her desk and read the letter again: the letter said that her benefits would end that month, so she would need to file (and pay) for COBRA for herself and her family. In a zombie-like state, Moira walked down the hall to say goodbye to her coworkers; some helped her find boxes to pack up her pictures, plants, and other belongings from her office.

Moira walked out to the parking lot with her two boxes and sat in her car, unsure what to do next. She had never been fired before. *Had* she been fired? She had already submitted her resignation. None of this made sense. With the consequences of this unexpected development starting to hit her, she called her husband to try to explain what had happened. "I can come to get you and help you get your stuff out of the office," he said, trying to comfort her. But Moira needed to sit and process a bit longer, and there was no reason to return to the office.

Moira went through a wild roller coaster of emotions sitting in that parking lot. She called a close lawyer friend to ask if what Jenny and Joe had done was legal. Moira's friend said it almost sounded like the letter had been started the moment Moira submitted her resignation, and Jenny and/or Joe were just looking for an excuse to fill in the blanks. In any case, it was unlikely that there would be a successful case. Like many things in that workplace, the actions were unethical and unfair but likely not illegal. Moira was angry, sad, ashamed, and felt a fool to have offered thirty days in her resignation. She felt a fool that, even after she received the termination letter, she had made sure she completed the list of transition items because she didn't want the grantees she worked with or her coworkers to suffer for this. Moira felt that a stain she couldn't remove had been smeared on her: *termination*. Even if no one ever knew, even if it was a vindictive technicality given that she'd already resigned, this was not something Moira had considered a possibility in her career.

As a woman of color, Moira felt that she always had to work harder, more creatively, and more impressively than others. She was always highly diplomatic in her written and spoken communications. She thought she had protected herself from being fired by working harder and smarter and being willing to leave the job rather than taking leadership head-on when the toxic culture became too much. But as Deepa Purushothaman says, "After a lifetime of over-functioning and overperforming, we end up disconnected, hypercritical of ourselves, and unable to lead from a place of authenticity and vision. We don't feel triumphant; instead, we feel stifled, isolated, and under extreme pressure."[1]

WHAT THIS EXPERIENCE CAN TEACH US

People who play these power games resort to vindictive, punishing, demeaning behavior toward anyone who refuses to engage in their game and acknowledge their power. Experiences such as this can also be understood within the frame of white backlash, which has long been a feature of U.S. culture and attempts to reframe efforts for racial justice as being "too far, too fast." As Lawrence Glickman describes in "How White Backlash Controls American Progress," white backlash is about the "elevation of [white] 'tranquility' over equal justice for all . . . which ranked white feelings over Black rights."[2]

This story teaches us not to trust words spoken by those in positions of power—*get it in writing*. Everything Moira had agreed to with Joe and Jenny was verbal; it was her word against theirs. *Get it in writing*. Many of the women I spoke to recounted situations in which they, in retrospect, were far too trusting. Many wished they had known better and documented the promises or inappropriate behavior instead of questioning themselves and their right-mindedness. Many of the women I spoke to had learned the hard way to negotiate for contracts, severance packages, and other safety nets when taking on new leadership positions.

Ask yourself: Does your organization have a policy addressing what to do when an employee transitions out? What benefits or compensation, if any, are provided in that transition? Any severance policy for health insurance transitions? How and with whom are exit letters shared? Are exit interviews a practice or a policy, and who conducts these interviews? How are transition plans carried out? Is there a policy about how long a notice employees should give? Do you know if you work in an at-will state? And don't forget about the crucial role that human resources ideally should play in creating a fair, trust-based, and collaborative workplace culture. Ensure that the organization's values are transparently reflected and enforced in human resources policies and practices, from job descriptions and postings to the hiring process to grievance processes, disciplinary action, to letting go or having an employee leave. *Get it in writing.*

CHAPTER 10

When White Women Do White Supremacy's Dirty Work

Moira's story from the previous chapter and the following story have a common theme that was brought up by every woman of color I spoke to: white women's relationship with white supremacy. In Moira's case, a white woman in a position of power, Jenny, was charged with carrying out and enforcing the CEO's decisions and creating a wall between staff and their boss, even though it was an organization with only eight staff. Even though Joe had decided to fire Moira, Jenny was the sole enforcer of his unreasonable and punitive decision. There's been a lot of public discourse in the last few years about white women and the role their particular intersection of gender and race plays in upholding white supremacy and patriarchy, and it is a necessary topic to engage with in creating healthy workplace cultures.

Alicia's story illustrates the potential cruelty of white women doing white supremacy and patriarchy's work. Alicia, an immigrant, began working at a local nonprofit while completing a graduate degree through a prestigious international fellowship. At the time of this story, she was transitioning from having a student visa to receiving a permanent resident card (green card). Alicia shared that her supervisor, a white woman, consistently engaged in a pattern of abusive and threatening behavior with her. Norma, Alicia's supervisor, knew that Alicia didn't have her green card yet, and she used that information to control Alicia. Alicia observed

Norma behave in ways that didn't seem ethical (particularly in Norma's interactions with other immigrant women of color), and she would approach Norma to express her concerns: "Norma, I just wanted to talk to you about the situation with the client we saw yesterday. I don't feel comfortable with your decision about her, and I hope we can explore other ways to provide her with the support she needs."

"Alicia, I know how important this job is to you, and I know you're in the process of getting your green card. I just want to ensure you have no trouble with that process." Alicia felt that Norma was threatening her: *Either go along with what I say, or I will make trouble for you, and you might lose your job and green card.*

Alicia told me, "Her abusive behavior was blatant. But I also had to wait for my green card, otherwise I couldn't work anywhere. And Norma knew this and used it to threaten me whenever I disagreed with her. And I never understood because I didn't have any problems with my coworkers, and I was getting recognition for my work at the local and state level. And that actually seemed to make her mad; the more recognition I got, the worse she treated me. She just couldn't believe that people would tell her that I was the expert on a certain topic and that she should come to me for guidance."

Alicia recalled having to get permission to attend all work-related meetings outside the office. When meetings were primarily about serving the immigrant community, Norma was unlikely to let her go. Alicia said the level of control and punitive behaviors became apparent to some of her white coworkers, who intervened on many occasions and even confronted Norma about the way she treated Alicia. Alicia reflected that in this job, she experienced white women upholding white supremacy and patriarchy through abusive behavior, but she also experienced white women using their privilege to call out and confront abuse and even give up a day off from work in order to stand in solidarity with Alicia (who was punished for something or other by being forced to work on a holiday when no one else was working).

A few months later, Alicia got her green card and decided that, even though she loved the work she did at the organization and especially loved working with Spanish-speaking clients, she had to quit the job because of the way Norma treated her and other immigrant women of color. Alicia gave one month's notice as she knew it would take a lot of work to set up a protocol for the new person to follow with so many cases of Spanish-speaking clients. Alicia wanted to set things up so that whoever they hired to take on her cases wouldn't create hardship for the women she worked with.

Alicia gave her one month's notice on a Monday, and on Wednesday Norma approached Alicia and said, "Alicia, this Friday is going to be your last day. And I'm sorry, but there's nothing you can say to change this, so please get everything in order today and tomorrow." As Alicia said, it was all about power and control.

It is important for white women to recognize their positionality and the power they wield within white supremacy. You can't skip straight into being an ally or accomplice without first acknowledging your power and relative privilege when working with women of color. As with Alicia's experience, white women can use their relative power and privilege to challenge the status quo and help move us collectively toward justice, or they can deny their relative privilege and power and be part of the oppressive systems that harm them and women of color. The following excerpt offers a way that an organizational leader worked within the existing inequitable system. In sharing this story, Laura acknowledged feeling saddened by having to resort to this approach, yet after trying other methods, she felt that this was a pragmatic way to deal with the reality of white supremacy in their work.

"And after years of working and trying different things to raise funds, we realized that our development person has to be a white woman if we want money from the bigger donors; it can't be a woman of color. That's what it takes to work with donors.

"We needed white women allies to work with on fundraising and contacts, donor engagement, and working with funders. We have found

*that it makes a big difference if we have white women with their gener-
ational wealth and contacts with access to money, privilege, and name
recognition working with us. That opened doors for our work, but it
had to include the privilege of white women. That's the reality we had
to work with, even though our organization is otherwise all Latinas."*

—LAURA, Latine nonprofit leader

WHAT THIS EXPERIENCE CAN TEACH US

*"Having white women question my right to be in positions of power and,
at times, even organize campaigns to discredit me."*

—Latine nonprofit leader survey participant

The issue of white women enacting white supremacy is particularly salient
in the philanthropic and nonprofit sectors because white women represent the largest demographic group in those workforces. In her article
"White Women Doing White Supremacy in Nonprofit Culture," Heather
Laine Talley created a list of "characteristics that I have both observed in
other white women and have participated in myself with insidious consequences." This list includes white women's tendency to "disavow power,"
their "obsession with the future" to the detriment of acknowledging and
investing in the here and now, "performative anti-racism," "overdeliver-
ing," "niceness above all else," and "confusing informality with equity."[1]

There are personal-level and organizational-level lessons in this story.
At the personal level, I strongly encourage white women who feel committed to practicing anti-racism or want to explore how white supremacy
has shaped their worldview and identity to read Laine Talley's article as a
starting point. I shared the article with several friends who are women of
color (and one white woman friend), and we all felt that it very accurately

88

represented our experiences with white women in the nonprofit, philanthropic, and academic sectors. Particularly (but not exclusively) for those working in philanthropy, I strongly recommend reading *White Women Cry and Call Me Angry* by Yanique Redwood. Yanique and I have known each other for many years, our work intersecting over the years within the philanthropic sector. It took nearly a decade of casual interactions before we shared with each other our stories of harm in philanthropy and the profound ways they affected our health and well-being. Being harmed can be very isolating, and for both of us, this isolation and the eventual realization that our experiences were tragically not rare inspired us to write about our experiences and help pull down the curtain of secrecy that conceals the rampant abuse in nonprofit and philanthropic workplaces.

When I read Yanique's book, the first thing that came to mind was how necessary it is for our collective healing to listen to and bear witness to the stories of Black women. To be witnesses to the myriad yet predictable ways that white-dominant workplaces have caused harm to Black women, Indigenous women, and other women of color, and how white women have been socialized to carry out the enforcement of these systems of oppression.

Do the work, and know that acknowledging the compounding barriers faced by women of color does not diminish the fact that patriarchy harms white women in profound ways; patriarchy harms all humans, regardless of gender, sex, or sexual orientation. Recognizing that white women have privileges not available to women of color does not negate the pain and barriers that white women experience due to sexism and misogyny. Do some reading about intersectionality, and don't limit your understanding to the "all women" argument, which makes the complex and compounded realities of Black, Indigenous, Brown, immigrant, and multiracial women invisible. This is not a zero-sum situation; the visibility of women of color does not obscure white women; creating spaces that value and support women of color will benefit everyone.

"I am not automatically given the same respect as a white male; people don't automatically assume I am a leader, that I have brains and a lot to bring to a table. I have to earn (and defend) respect and my position and face more challenges to my authority and leadership than others, simply because of who I am. I am also physically disabled, which adds another layer of intersectionality."

—Asian American survey participant

At the core of understanding the lived experiences of women of color is understanding intersectionality. Intersectionality acknowledges multiple identities, experiences, and positionality. I highly encourage you to read writings by and about Kimberlé Crenshaw.[2] Much has been written about intersectionality, and much has been expressed and misunderstood about it. *The Intersectionality Resource Guide and Toolkit* by United Nations Women calls intersectionality "an approach, a mindset" and provides a useful introduction and resources for any organization wanting to understand and put intersectionality into practice.[3] Learning new and challenging concepts and perspectives as an ongoing practice allows us—as individuals and organizations—to move from defensiveness to curiosity. Prioritize learning about intersectionality, and move beyond binary understandings of identity.

Silence and Inaction as Harm

CHAPTER 11

You Just Sound So Confident and Competent

White supremacy convinces white people that they are smart and right, and anything that makes them feel otherwise must be bad and must be stopped

Much has been written about white fragility and how white supremacy creates frailty in those who identify as white when it comes to anything that questions, challenges, or makes visible the unearned privilege and entitlement of whiteness.[1] Black and Brown women are often told they are strong, intense, and passionate—comments that skate close to the many racialized tropes about each of these perceived behaviors. The truth is that when women of color use their "strength and intensity" to speak up against the status quo, it is called anger and emotionality, and the woman is labeled intimidating, scary, unprofessional, out of control, or disloyal. The following stories are examples of how white fragility manifests in workplaces for women of color.

Yulia: The Fear of Strong Women of Color

Yulia shared a story about how a wealthy, white, male board member told her she was *scary*: "You're a scary woman. You are smart, confident, and courageous. I mean . . .!" There was no self-awareness in his statement.

She didn't know how to respond to this comment, so she forced a perplexed smile as she walked away from this older, white, wealthy man who held power as a member of her organization's board. His words spun in her head: *You're scary.* Yulia understood what he meant: *Your power scares me.*

"If this toned-down, restrained, professional version of me is scary, how can I ever bring my full self into the work I care about so much?," Yulia told me. "If my strength, intelligence, and power are viewed as scary by those who hold power and resources at the place where I work, what does that mean for how I lead? How can I lead? If a board member views me as scary, am I considered dangerous?"

Mia: Persistent Tone-Policing of Women of Color

A similar story comes from Mia, also involving a privileged, white, male board member. This board member, Parker, spoke to Mia about why some board members were upset with her. In the kindest and most sincere tone (and Mia believes he said this with every intention of being helpful), Parker said, "Sometimes when you speak at meetings, you sound so confident and competent, so sure of yourself, that it makes some of our board members uncomfortable."

Trying to focus on Parker's intention, not his words, Mia asked him: "Parker, what would you do in my place when a decision is being made based on incorrect information or assumptions? I see it as an important part of my job to provide correct information and to say something when incorrect information gets into our decision-making."

Parker pondered, then said, "I don't know. I understand why you want decisions made with correct information, of course, but I know that your presence at meetings, your competence, and confidence make some uncomfortable. I know you don't mean to do that, and that's why I wanted to let you know. Maybe you could address the incorrect information after the meeting, in private, so no one feels like you're correcting them?"

Mia understood the message. There was no practical way to wait until after the meeting when a decision was being made—decisions at board meetings meant taking a vote, and waiting until after a vote would be impractical, complicated, and absurd.

Yulia's and Mia's stories take me back to being a child and being told by adults that, as a girl, I shouldn't try to sound too intelligent or confident because it would be off-putting to men. Or the adolescent version where adults told me, "Too bad you're so tall, you won't be able to wear high heels; you don't want to be taller than men." The message has loudly been: don't be too smart, don't be too confident, don't be so tall, make yourself small so you won't scare those in power. If you step into your power, you will seem dangerous, scary, and intimidating—*unseemly*.

Organizations hire specific women of color as leaders for lots of reasons: because she's smart and creative; because she has relevant lived experience; because she has a vision that she is willing to act upon; for her extensive education; for her deep and impressive work experience; for her nuanced understanding of the issues. The same people who hire her too often flip from fetishizing her to resenting her, getting mad at her, and mistreating her because they can't believe that she dares show her intelligence, confidence, and vision in her work.

Courage is sexy until it is used to challenge the status quo that upholds *power over*. This is a painfully common theme in conversations with women of color leaders, possibly the most common one. In my career, I have often been hired to bring about change and then attacked and undermined because change doesn't *feel* the way those in power thought it would. *Change means change.*

These attitudes appear throughout all the stories shared by the women I spoke to. Repeatedly, women of color are told they are (too) angry, intense, scary, intimidating, full of themselves, confident, big, and bold. *Too much.*

WHAT THIS EXPERIENCE CAN TEACH US

Supremacist cultures create fragile egos, entitled and conditioned to feel special and important and benefit from the unearned spotlight and praise. When you are used to being praised for being just as you are, when you're raised to see yourself as the presumed leader and knower, making space for others' ways of knowing and being is difficult. Entitlement is a result of consistently being told (implicitly and explicitly) that you have a right to _____. Society feels comfortable, natural, and right to those who identify and are perceived as white. The less proximate you are to being white, male, cisgendered, and Christian, the less comfortable, natural, or right society feels.

As demographics change and as recognition grows that diverse teams are more creative and effective, white patriarchy seduces women of color into organizations that need change and need to look more diverse. Once women of color are in positions of leadership, organizations gag them, demean and threaten them, gaslight them, and undermine them precisely because of the courage, boldness, and determination that living as a woman of color in a white-supremacist patriarchy demands of us.

These stories illustrate what the Safehouse Progressive Alliance for Nonviolence has termed the Problem Woman of Color in a Nonprofit.[2] This tool illustrates in shocking simplicity my own experience and the experiences of the dozens of women of color I have spoken to and who participated in the survey for this book:

- Honeymoon phase: Woman of color is wooed and enters the organization.

- The reality of racism in the organization becomes apparent: WOC points out concerns and tries to change systems. The organization denies any claims by WOC and puts the responsibility and blame onto individual WOC while pitting people of color against each other and centering white leadership styles.

- WOC exits the organization: Harm is done to WOC, and the organization experiences no accountability.

> *"All of a sudden, I'm a troublemaker."*
>
> —KRISTA, Black nonprofit leader

This dynamic has also been referred to as going "from pet to threat" by Kecia M. Thomas.[3] In her article "When Black Women Go from Office Pet to Office Threat,"[4] Erika Stallings shares examples of Black women's experiences with this phenomenon. Her stories echo much of what I heard from the women I spoke to for this book and the dozens of conversations I have had with friends and colleagues who are women of color working in leadership roles. This toxic pattern is shockingly common. Across the U.S., across race and ethnicity among women of color, and across nonprofit, philanthropic, and academic workplaces. There is a structural default setting to treat women of color in the workplace in this way: pet to threat or as a (capital P) Problem. An Asian American survey participant shared in response to what barriers she has faced as a leader: *"Pet-to-threat: board and other superiors are enamored by who/what they think I represent, but when I demonstrate power, they don't like it."*

An additional dynamic at play for many of the women I spoke to is what Vu Le has named the *outsider efficacy bias*. As described by Le in his Nonprofit AF blog, "We have a rampant belief in our sector that people from outside our organization/community/geographic area are somehow more knowledgeable and effective than the people in it."[5] For many of the women I interviewed and myself, organizations hire us because of our expertise and experiences, yet too often, once we become an internal and familiar agent, our expertise is no longer trusted or desired.

Stories I heard all went like this: Woman of color is invited in, arms wide open with great excitement and bold visions of change, and always with much publicity by the organization, congratulating itself for hiring a woman of color. But as she begins to implement change-making decisions, transform cultural practices, and make assumptions evident, resistance starts up. Criticism is first targeted at ideas and practices. Criticisms then turn toward the woman of color, not the ideas, and the more uncomfortable that people with the most historical power feel, the more dissatisfaction, fear, and anger become personalized. Because women of color often find themselves as the only or one of the few questioning the status quo and making the unspoken power dynamics visible, their perspective is seen as dangerous, uninformed, biased, or unimportant. Women of color are intentionally excluded from organizational decisions and then blamed for disconnects. Discomfort is misread as a danger because of white supremacy's right to comfort, and, so predictably, the woman of color—*who was hired to bring about change*—is vilified; the only solution considered is to squelch her fire or get rid of her.

And these dynamics don't get better in senior leadership roles. As Gail Christopher and Deepa Iyer write, "When they do attain leadership roles, challenges persist; the intersectional threats posed by patterns of misogyny and racism intensify, rather than lessen. Leadership roles involve increased responsibility, accountability, and potential risks for all people. For women of color stepping into leadership circles historically dominated by white men, the heightened risks include diminishment, harassment, prejudice, and inadequate support." Further, speaking to this particular moment, "women of color leaders have expressed that the current climate—marked by the COVID-19 pandemic, racial reckoning, and organizational challenges—has taken an immeasurable toll on their psychological, physical, and emotional well-being."[6]

Every woman I spoke to had experienced a story that followed this general pattern, and it was never an isolated incident or story. The pattern repeats so predictably. This is not an individual problem; this is a structural issue with how we've constructed our notions and models for leadership, organizations, and how to bring about change. This is a problem of power and its misapplication within the context of layered historical injustices and patterns of violence. This is an issue of the inherent and relentless violence and injustice of patriarchy and white supremacy and their vile, co-dependent marriage.

"And maybe being made to feel small, less than, and making us question ourselves. That piece is destroying me lately because I had an experience with that this week. I was talking to a good friend of mine last night and saying how at this point in my career, in my life, with the accomplishments I have, with the evidence I have around me, I still walk away from meeting with my board members feeling like I'm a fraud like I messed up. Like I don't know what I'm doing, like I don't know how I got this far. I'm an idiot.

I mean, just how can that still be happening? It's a lot. And I think that's why many of us (women of color) leave. I've had many conversations with women of color in leadership positions who are like; I don't know how much longer I want to do this. I don't know how much longer I can *do this. Because their families tell them, as my family tells me, 'You got to take care of yourself.' These experiences leave the body very beaten up."*

—ALEJANDRA, Latine philanthropic leader

If an organization, or the leadership of an organization, is telling a woman of color (explicitly or implicitly) to make herself small, to mind her tone, to diminish her shine, to mind her place because she's scary when her courage shows, *that place is toxic.*

We should never feel that our work requires us to make ourselves small.

We should not have to accept attacks on our dignity at work.

We should never have to bare our scars and pain to be treated humanely or contort ourselves to be acceptable to those with power over us.

Pay attention to comments about women of color's tone, demeanor, and strength. Listen for a version of "Who does she think she is?" Or anything along the lines of "She's so angry, scary, intimidating" (or in the honeymoon phase, "so passionate, so fiery, so bold").

Pay attention to how you implement expectations of "professionalism" in your organization. Are expectations skewed toward a specific culture, identity, or population? Suppose your organization is thinking about recruiting a leader of color or already has a leader of color. Do culture work with your board and staff to become aware of how white-dominant culture might be showing up and creating unrealistic, unfair, and irrelevant expectations and models of what leadership and professionalism look and sound like. Sida Ly-Xiong recommends organizations ask themselves these questions to prepare for and to support leaders working to change structures and systems:

- What changes do we seek? How are we currently making decisions related to these changes? To what extent are we, individually and collectively, willing to take responsibility for real change?

- What is at risk if we do or do not implement change? Can we acknowledge the tension between those risks and accept growing pains as important and necessary? What support do we need to foster a culture of learning, risk, and mutual vulnerability?

- Are we willing to investigate others' beliefs and narratives about us, even if they challenge our assumptions about our organization's identity, purpose, and impact? What new narratives do we need to embrace transformative leadership?

- To what extent do we understand how privilege is embedded in our organizational norms and cultural contexts? Are we willing to increase transparency and make our decision-making processes more inclusive?[7]

CHAPTER 12

Complicit Silence

Allyship means speaking out, even— and especially—if it rocks the boat

Most people are not consciously prone to intentional cruelty or abusive behavior. Yet many of those not-cruel, not-abusive people are perfectly comfortable remaining silent in the face of abuse and cruelty, rationalizing and justifying, which is a huge boon for white supremacy. The stories in this section are particularly easy to ignore or misread. Hiding behind white guilt (a strange manifestation of racism that excuses guilt-ridden white individuals from speaking up in situations where they should say something), some people take no action yet see the inaction as proof of innocence.

From board members sharing with their executive director that they would never be able to work in the conditions that the executive director has to work under, but then keeping silent when other board members behave in ways that they would find unacceptable in their own organizations; to peers or board members who approach women of color after meetings to tell them they agree with them, after keeping silent during heated arguments in a meeting: *white silence in the face of harm is harm itself*. Those frozen in white guilt must find courage and a way toward proactive white allyship. The stories that follow seem particularly illustrative of the theme of complicit silence.

Naomi: The Harm Caused by Conflict Avoidance

Naomi knew it would be challenging to serve as CEO of an organization following the founding CEO's retirement. In addition to the already significant culture shift from founding leader to second leader, the founding CEO was a white man. Naomi is a woman of color and younger than him. Naomi did not, however, expect the viciousness of the exchanges among board members during board meetings. Within months, the animosity started to be directed at Naomi, too. But Naomi was focused on navigating the COVID-19 pandemic as a new leader at the organization. Although the dynamics with the board were challenging, things needed to get done, so she brought in consultants to help work with the board, hoping this would generate solutions to bring some calm to interactions with and among board members. But after the board repeatedly fired consultants when they didn't agree with them, Naomi's hope shifted to concern and then, amid the relentless work during the pandemic, shifted to learned helplessness.

The dynamics with the board went from bad to worse to deeply toxic. Individually, most board members seemed to be lovely people, but something about the group together made for gut-wrenching interactions and vitriolic exchanges. After a particular board meeting, two board members, who were CEOs of their own organizations, approached Naomi:

Liz, a middle-aged white woman who'd attended Ivy League schools, cornered Naomi and said, "I would never be able to put up with behavior like this on my board. I don't know how you do it. I've never seen anything like this!"

Another board member, Phil, executive director of a nonprofit, also alum of Ivy League universities, called Naomi later that afternoon to express empathy for her predicament. "I do feel for you, Naomi. I'm so sorry about the way the board behaved today. I can't imagine having to work under those conditions."

Yet these same board members failed to speak up at the board meeting when individuals behaved in ways that any reasonable person would deem deeply inappropriate. Neither Phil nor Liz interrupted direct attacks on Naomi or her staff at the meeting. They commiserated with Naomi as a peer privately but kept silent during heated exchanges at meetings. Board meetings prioritized the comfort of those with positional power.

In prioritizing conflict avoidance and relationships with peer board members, Liz and Phil allowed their peers to disregard and disrespect Naomi and other staff members.

Kayla: The Cost of Speaking Up

Kayla, who had been working at an organization for over a year, had observed what she believed to be inappropriate behavior, specifically incidents of racism and sexism in the workplace. After consulting the personnel policy handbook, Kayla followed organizational policy, went to the human resources (HR) representative, and shared her concerns. Kayla felt she had done the right thing, and while she was anxious about the whole situation, she was comfortable with her decision to go to HR about what she'd observed.

To her dismay, within a week of her conversation with HR, Kayla was asked to leave the organization, with a generous package offered. She was baffled. Kayla tried to speak to her supervisor, Cindy, with whom she'd always had a reasonably good relationship, to understand what was happening. Cindy, however, had been instructed not to communicate with Kayla. So despite Cindy having no reason to want Kayla to leave and no negative reviews of Kayla's work, Cindy complied with HR's instructions and never spoke to Kayla again or gave Kayla an explanation. Kayla felt that this was done, in part, to send a message to others: don't rock the boat, don't talk about racism or sexism. And Cindy's complicit silence strengthened that message. Kayla left the organization and never again heard from Cindy.

Mariana: The Omnipotence of White Comfort

Mariana shared a frustrating story about a project she had been working on for nearly a year before the metaphorical plug was pulled. Mariana was part of a steering committee working on various community engagement efforts. She had been leading the planning and preparation for an engagement effort with the Latinx community. For months, she had been sharing her plans and progress with the group of almost entirely white participants, who seemed mostly disinterested in the project, other than to repeatedly ask: "Why is this project only for Latinos? Shouldn't it be more inclusive?"

"Actually, the purpose of this project is to specifically look at issues facing our Latinx community," Mariana explained. "The project certainly doesn't intend to exclude others. It has been designed with the specific context of the Latinx community in mind due to disproportionate unmet needs we have identified."

A couple of days later, Mariana received a call from an unknown number, and it turned out to be the organization's president. She did not work directly with the president and had never received a call from him on her cell phone. "Hi, Mariana, it's so good to get a chance to speak with you. First, I just want to say how much I appreciate your work. I know the work you do, especially with the community, is so important, and I see your commitment, and I want you to know how committed I am to supporting you." She was trying to decipher the rest of the conversation, as it was peppered with statements about things being done a particular way at the organization, about not wanting to veer into uncomfortable territory, and, of course, he supported her and appreciated her work. He wanted to be viewed as a big proponent of diversity, and made sure she understood that.

The president wanted Mariana to know that she could reach out to him and that she was valued, but what Mariana heard was: *Don't push any further. Don't advocate. Don't challenge. You don't need to know or ask why.* When the call from the president ended, she felt confused . . . as if someone had just slapped her while wearing a smile.

The steering committee members never said a word about the project Mariana had been working on, and it never got on the agenda again.

WHAT THIS EXPERIENCE CAN TEACH US

During a recent conversation with me, my teenage son was reflecting on things he'd learned through playing sports, and one of the lessons he was most surprised by but also really loved was that *lack of action is, in and of itself, an action, and can be used as part of the broader strategy.* He realized that nonactions (standing still, blocking, not passing) were just as much of the game's strategy as the actions (running, passing, etc.). In the workplace, choosing not to do something is also a decision, a nonaction that conveys values, assumptions, and worldviews. He had cracked the truth that leadership is about what you do and say *and* what you don't do and don't say. In the preceding stories, the various holders of positional power chose to ignore this and pretended that not saying something meant they were not guilty of the egregious behavior they had witnessed. But protecting comfort and superficial politeness—upholding a pretense of perfection at the expense of the dignity of those harmed—will not lead us to collective liberation.

If you have found yourself in similar situations, ask yourself why you chose to act or not act. If you kept quiet, what did you feel, and what did you think at the time? Do this with curiosity, not shame. Understanding why you didn't act will help you find ways to interrupt the lack of action. Read about being an ally. Allyship in the workplace is "a strategic mechanism used by individuals to become collaborators, accomplices, and coconspirators who fight injustice and promote equity in the workplace through supportive personal relationships and public acts of sponsorship and advocacy. Allies endeavor to drive systemic improvements to workplace policies, practices, and culture," according to sociologist Tsedale M. Melaku and colleagues.[1] Educate yourself about what being an ally means, and practice—intentionally and regularly—speaking up when you sense or realize that something is off, someone is being treated unfairly, or someone is abusing their power.

I am not asking you to intervene in armed conflict; I am simply suggesting that you acknowledge what you've witnessed and say something if you wouldn't want to be treated that way or if you know the person(s) on the receiving end of the behavior doesn't want to be treated that way. This is also how we change culture. We make it clear that certain behaviors are not acceptable and that there will be consequences—even if it is just someone saying, "That's not an acceptable behavior."

On being an ally, my children have also reflected—after enduring what they experienced as a surreal school presentation on being an ally that transparently centered the experience and perspective of white-identified individuals—that being an ally is just basically being a decent human being.

Stand-alone trainings or organizational branding cannot take the place of values-based policies and structures that create conditions for values-aligned behaviors and practices. Developing policies based on shared and explicit organizational values should be the foundation for creating a healthy culture. And by organizational values, I am referring to shared social norms, group expectations, and shared principles that define an organization's purpose and what it is working toward, such that organizational members can easily identify and speak out when shared values are violated. To build accountability without devolving into punitive measures, keep organizational values alive by doing exercises with the board and staff every year, develop group norms or community commitments with your team and board, and implement mechanisms and tools for enforcing these agreements. Remember that creating community agreements and values alone is not enough; you have to actively and consistently practice and assess them.

CHAPTER 13

I'll Just Take Equity Out!

And the harm that man-child leaders cause at work

Ana: The Thin Skin of White Male Privilege

During a staff meeting, the full team of a policy-focused organization discussed how to approach a policy issue they had been working on for years: whether to support legislation that would regulate and limit smoking tobacco in public spaces. Everyone knew that no matter what the organization did, it would inevitably make someone unhappy. Its partner organizations and the research they had sponsored stood on the same side the organization had taken for nearly a decade: supporting tobacco-free legislation and significantly restricting public smoking. The one thing that had changed recently was that the incoming governor opposed this policy, so publicly supporting tobacco-free legislation alongside their community partners would pin the organization on the opposite side from the governor's administration.

As policy lead for the organization, Ana spoke for the staff, who all felt it was important to stick with their long-held position, supported by partners, community leaders, and research. The organization was non-partisan and based its policy positions on research. The staff believed that because their organization didn't depend on the state for funding, it had an important and unique position to take a bold stance on this central policy issue. Ana's boss, Chad, didn't agree: "That's naïve. We have to pay attention to who is on our side and who's against us. We don't want to be on the side of those who will lose on this issue."

Ana presented an argument for sticking with the current position based on an equity analysis of the situation (a key part of her role at the organization) and then reiterated, "And our mission clearly states that equity is central to our work." She explained to Chad, who had not been in the CEO position very long, that using an equity analysis for decisions was a practice the staff had developed to test their positions and decisions against their mission whenever a question arose.

Chad leaned forward, slammed one hand onto the table, raised his voice, waved his other hand as if to swat down an annoying fly, and said, "I've had enough of this nonsense; we're moving on."

The staff was caught in a momentary awkward silence, sharing glances, their expressions communicating their dismay. Supporting tobacco-free policy approaches was central to the organization's work and their organizational partners. The staff had been reminding Chad for weeks that they had to come up with a path forward together so they could communicate clearly with their research and community partners.

Ana spoke: "Chad, we realize this is a difficult situation, but there is a clear answer when we look at our mission, our historical position, the research we've funded, and our policy decision tree. This is also extremely time-sensitive, so we feel we must decide today."

This enraged Chad, who had let it be known in previous staff meetings that having a position or perspective different from his was equivalent to attacking him. A few staff members had started speaking when Chad raised his voice at Ana, turned red in the face, waved his arms in the air, and shouted:

"If you don't stop talking about equity, I will take the damn word out of the mission statement and be done with it. I am tired of this!"

With those words, a policy discussion at work turned personal, and (abusive) power, threats, and anger were used to silence Ana. A couple of staff were shaking their heads while most others cast their heads down, avoiding making eye contact with anyone. Ana was one of two people of color in the organization. Chad was one of two men; the other man was significantly younger than Chad. Additionally, Chad had preexisting relationships with most board members, being from a family of wealth and legacy political power in the state.

Although she was working at a mission-driven organization, Ana was not allowed to do her work guided by the mission. Chad viewed equity as an annoyance, and Ana was the primary champion of this annoyance. The fact that she was willing to engage Chad even when he tried to intimidate her and other staff with yelling, physical posturing, and frequent reminders that he was the boss—and that she didn't back down or act hurt by Chad's behavior—made him even more enraged with her.

As with too many other women of color in majority-white spaces, Ana ended up leaving after realizing that Chad was not willing to engage in mature, constructive interactions, that sufficient other staff were willing to go along with him, stay quiet, or keep their head down to avoid his outbursts, and that she would never be free of his abusive behavior if she stayed. Prior to leaving, Ana tried reaching out to a couple of board members: one never responded, and the other met with her, truly concerned and outraged. This board member, however, felt disempowered to do anything. He had raised concerns at board meetings and questioned decisions made by Chad, only to be chastised and silenced by both Chad and fellow board members who benefited from Chad's ballooning power and connections outside of work. Ana shared that even after multiple staff left, even though staff with long tenure and leadership positions at the organization spoke up and shared concerns about Chad's behavior with the board, Chad remained in the same position, even years later. Meanwhile, Chad's salary increased, and the organization's impact diminished.

WHAT THIS EXPERIENCE CAN TEACH US

Power over people is oppressive; it smothers creativity and innovation and infuses organizational culture with fear and distrust. It's hard to have integrity in your work when it is filtered through the preferences of a thin-skinned, entitled person prone to temper tantrums. Yet this was a common theme in my interviews with women of color leaders. In this case, white supremacy was paired with unabashed patriarchy, leading to ideological bullying, stagnation, and suppression of values-aligned ideas. This experience also illustrates the deeply racialized and gendered perceptions of behavior—had a woman exhibited the same behavior as Chad, she would have been called hysterical and unstable; a person of color would have been called aggressive, dangerous, and unprofessional. The notion of a sole, unquestionable hero-leader is a supremacist and patriarchal notion, and it becomes self-perpetuating.

To prevent harm and a culture of fear, we must create checks and balances and distribute decision-making power within our institutions and organizations. For example, codifying decision-making processes is essential to transparency and accountability. Having clear, written, and accessible grievance processes is essential to preventing, reporting, and addressing abuse of power. Finally, conflict-of-interest policies for boards need to be handled with care and thoughtful consideration, to prevent board membership being treated as a reward for those who go along to get along or as part of an informal quid pro quo among people with power and influence.

There are too many stories to recount of board members who saw their allegiance as being to the influential and well-connected CEO or fellow board member rather than to the organization's mission. Conflict of interest gets emphasized in direct receipt of funds from one entity to another (for example, some foundations have rules against grantee organizations serving on their boards, thereby missing out on important and relevant perspectives and experiences), but the less formal relationships of mutual benefit among people of power are not scrutinized in the same way—yet were a common theme in the conversations I had while researching this book.

CHAPTER 14

The Added Burden and Toll of Unpaid and Unseen Emotional Labor

"How have women of color worked to be legitimate in their workplaces? How has it served them and hurt them? What is the cost of proving and working toward legitimacy?"

—SOLEDAD, Latine philanthropic leader

During the interviews I conducted for this book, a theme present in each one was feeling drained by the emotional labor at work. Conversations about the added burden of emotional labor by women of color in the workplace included stories about having to remain calm and smile through repeated insults, offensive remarks, and microaggressions; enduring stereotypes, and racialized and gendered tropes; stories about white women's weaponized tears and passive-aggressiveness; feeling both invisible and hyper-visible; having to do racial equity work even if it isn't part of their job; the unspoken expectation that women of color will do all the work of their position and also be an emotional caregiver for the organization.

A 2018 report by Catalyst explores the concept of an *emotional tax* at work: "Emotional Tax is the combination of feeling different from peers at work because of gender, race, and/or ethnicity and the associated effects on health, well-being, and ability to thrive at work. These experiences can be particularly acute for people of color who fear being stereotyped, receiving unfair treatment, or feeling like the 'other' (i.e., set apart from colleagues because of some aspect of their identity such as gender, race, or ethnicity)."[1] As Danielle, a Black nonprofit leader, said when describing the internal dialogue happening about how she is perceived when she exercises her embodied power as a leader, *"All of that is evaluated through implicit bias, through the tropes and the stereotypes of strong Black women, Black women who climbed the ladders . . . the angry Black woman trope . . . We still navigate our insecurities; we question how Black can I be in that space, right? The hair issues, the tone of our voices, and how loud we are."*

A lifetime of being marginalized can have uniquely potent effects, including on health and well-being. According to the study cited in the Catalyst report, women of color are the group most likely to "be on guard" and to anticipate gender and racial bias at work. Code-switching, constantly translating across cultures and worldviews, and filtering ourselves for our safety and others' comfort are exhausting.

Yet even in the context of this added emotional labor, women of color find ways to adapt and intensify their resolve. An interesting finding of the study cited in the Catalyst report is that

> the ability to consciously prepare for potential bias may enable some people to persevere, particularly when they recognize that the bias affecting them is external and changeable—rather than due to some inner flaw. Indeed, experiencing difficult situations may foster purpose and resolve in the face of adversity. Asian, Black, and Latinx respondents who report higher levels of being on guard also report more creativity (81%)—the ability to demonstrate originality and try out new approaches or processes at work—than those experiencing lower levels of being on guard (64%). Asian, Black, and Latinx respondents who report higher levels of being on guard are also more likely (79%) to report speaking up, e.g., when something needs to be said or when something happens that is not seen as appropriate, than those experiencing lower levels of being on guard (62%).[2]

As a multiracial (Latine, Asian American) survey participant shared: *"What about the informal leadership roles that WOC have in organizations? WOCs have the best 'soft' skills yet are taken for granted in organizations. For example, carrying the emotional burden of workplace drama, relational connection, and customer service."*

Paradoxically, it is in part because we've faced so many systemic barriers to reaching leadership roles that women of color are such creative, adaptive, and courageous leaders. In the words of Lucia, a Latine educational leader, women of color's lived experiences navigating visible and invisible barriers equip them to *"question everything from policies to programming to structures and keep what is useful to more than simply a minority of people with power and move forward with what potentially could be more nurturing to everyone, including those who haven't had leadership positions."*

This Is Personal

An important dimension of emotional labor for many women of color is that the issues they are working on are not just professional or abstract; they are personal and high-stakes. As Krista, a Black nonprofit leader said, *"We're close to the issues, and we're close to the suffering, we're close to the pain."* Every woman I spoke to, and many of those surveyed, talked about the emotional effort of restraint in responding to comments that (especially white) people make to them regularly. As Angela, Black nonprofit leader, said, *"I mean, to be told you're scary, you're intimidating, you make people feel bad by your sheer existence, like what does that do to your ability to exert your power, to be a leader? It makes me question myself: Is it me? Am I this person they're describing? And then I do this emotional and mental exploration."* The demands on emotional labor are not confined to situations when women of color must deal with individuals who openly undermine or attack women of color leaders. Women shared that both people they saw as allies and those who were transparently undermining them created conditions that required additional emotional labor. For example, *"What was so hard about it was—people who loved me and said they respected me replicated the status quo of oppression by encouraging me to conform rather than teach me more effective code-switching, negotiation, and translation skills." —Multiracial community leader survey participant*

Tait Manning writes about this and says,

> Women of Color are expected to control, modify, and suppress emotions in ways that white people, and to a different extent, Men of Color are not. We either conceal or redefine them to make our presence more palatable for the comfort of others. Modifying language, cultural references, identity, and behavior to conform to standards outside one's job responsibilities is tiring and burdensome for Women of Color within your organizations. This struggle is further complicated in professional workplaces where women of color are even more likely to be outnumbered by white people and men. The constant managing of emotions, enduring various forms of discrimination, being forced to code-switch to be taken seriously, and being exploited and tokenized requires a lot of emotional labor on the part of Women of Color.[3]

Many of the women I interviewed and surveyed mentioned having to restrain themselves to filter what they bring to the workplace. Krista, a Black nonprofit leader, felt that she is never viewed as talking, walking, or behaving in the way that workplaces consider appropriate for a leader. She explained: *"Typically, our goals [as women of color] differ. How we show up is different, how we respond is different, our level of passion is different, and what's at stake for us is different. What I've experienced is that when it's a Black woman who's being uncompromising, she's being a bitch, she's being angry, she's not being like whatever she is supposed to be. No! We don't have time to compromise! We're dying. There's a different level of urgency and reality [for women of color]."*

The concept of emotional labor was a theme alive in all interviews and survey responses, and it is a major burden (and energy drain) in my personal experience. Working within a culture that doesn't account for or create space for one's reality, experiences, and identity is exhausting. When asked about the primary obstacles they've faced at work, the women who participated in my survey for this book recounted the following as contributing to the added emotional labor:

- Lack of respect and lack of support

- Exclusion from opportunities

- Awareness that white coworkers are paid significantly/disproportionately more

- Constant scrutiny and second-guessing

- Feeling undervalued and underestimated

- Tokenism and fetishizing of women of color ("pet to threat" was explicitly named)

- Expectation to represent all women of color or specific community (all Latines, all Asian Americans, all Black people, and so forth); one survey respondent referred to "rep sweats"—a term coined by stand-up comic Jenny Yang to describe the reality that people of color often feel like they have to represent their entire race or community and the pressure that puts on an individual.[4]

- Lack of understanding of intersectional identities at work

- Pressure to be "flawless," better than others, and to overproduce

- Being told they are intimidating, scary, angry, loud, unprofessional

- Constant code-switching

- Lack of mentorship

- Gaslighting (this was also named in every interview)

Regarding the expectation to represent one's entire community(ies), women I interviewed and surveyed mentioned their commitment to support other women of color, while also recognizing that this layered on an additional level of responsibility and work—something that white men and women don't face, as there are so many more white leaders to serve as mentors, as well as mentorship programs geared toward whiteness and white leadership.

> *"The added labor we carry to mentor younger WOC and/or support our POC colleagues. Basically, to reach back down and pull other WOC up."*
>
> —Black nonprofit leader survey participant

Say My Name

Being denied your name is a particularly demoralizing microaggression. Navigating situations where you are denied your name takes a lot of emotional labor; over a lifetime, this extra work adds up. This denial comes in many forms, from mispronouncing and anglicizing names, to flat-out having white people say they won't say your name and giving you a name of their choosing, to being addressed with more informality than others in your position.

Danielle, a Black nonprofit leader, talked about the frustration of being in public events where white men were called by an honorific while she was referred to by her first name, although they had the same title. Given that women of color in leadership are disproportionately educated, several women talked about not being referred to as "Dr." while white and male peers were. Danielle shared an experience where she noticed a very real shift in how white people treated her when she introduced herself with "Dr." in front of her name: *"I had Doctor in front of my name, and these older white people shifted their behavior toward me . . . just before, the same people had been very rough with me . . . it changed how they talked to me . . . it was a shift in the atmosphere . . . it was very noticeable and part of noticing it is also being like, how do I feel about this?"*

For immigrant women and women of color with names that are not familiar to or comfortable for white people, this quote from Lucia, a Latine educational leader, is illustrative: *"Not taking the time for something as simple as how to say your name, because they see it as so outside of their frame of reference that they don't think they need to even try to do that in a way that they would with anyone else to show respect and to show recognition. So having someone in a higher rank position tell me that my name is not easy enough to pronounce, so they just won't say it, and not understand that's both offensive and out of line, shows just how much some identities are not accepted. Not even recognized as being able to take up space in certain areas of leadership."*

Our names reflect our stories and histories, cultures, languages, and ancestors and are an essential way we manifest our identities. Many women I interviewed shared stories of their names being changed, ignored, or ridiculed, particularly by board members and others in positions of power. Veronica's story is representative of situations that many women shared with me: *"All of a sudden, the chair of the board of trustees and the most powerful person in the room came up to us and started small talk. She said something to the person next to me, then turned to me and said, 'Oh, I'm going to introduce you before you give your remarks. So how do you say your name?'*

"I said my last name, and she looked at me and turned, laughing, to the white woman next to me and said, 'Why can't you have a name like her (pointing to the white woman)? That's an easy one.' I was horrified, and I had a young intern beside me, whose name is also 'foreign-sounding,' and she looked horrified. At that moment, I knew that because of this person's power, I couldn't really react, but I had to do something while knowing that because of her power, this could realistically affect my job and my family if I lost my job."

Everyone who mentioned an incident with their name being mispronounced, avoided, or changed said the same thing: I understand that not everyone can accurately pronounce my name; I don't expect everyone to be able to say it well on the first try or maybe even ever. All I am asking is that if someone doesn't know how to pronounce my name, they should ask me and try. *That's it.* It's a small effort with deep significance.[5] Next time you encounter someone whose name you don't know how to pronounce, ask them how to say their name, then try to say it, and then try again.

All the Feels

People of color (especially Black people) carry a disproportionate burden for emotional labor at work.[6] This includes leading the work on equity, inclusion, and diversity at work even when it's not part of their job, experiencing a higher degree of microaggressions (the concrete ceiling for women of color[7]), a lack of support, and gaslighting. Doing emotional labor adds insult to the fact that too many workplace cultures undermine women of color's ability to live healthy, balanced lives and build intergenerational wealth. By extension, those workplaces are harming our broader communities. And emotional labor is not just for women of color in staff positions. The following story was shared by a Latine nonprofit leader survey participant about her service on a board: *"Being a woman of color, it is seldom that we are given the power to make decisions and lead in the ways that we think are important. I just quit a board where I had no power, and what I suggested was either not heard, not understood, and, of course, never embraced. Sometimes, an idea would be snatched from me and appropriated by others. However, my ideas, vision, and perspective were often ignored or questioned before being dismissed. I finally resigned, and the amount of head and emotional space freed up is amazing! I had all it takes to influence and lead the organization into necessary and beneficial change. Still, I had no power to materialize my vision of collaboration, creativity, and inclusion. Now the board is, once again, all white."*

Emotional labor is a significant, pervasive, and complex reality shared by every woman I interviewed and surveyed; it was also a dimension of every other theme identified through the interviews and surveys. Through the stories shared with me and my own experiences, I understand the emotional toll to be the result of having to navigate intentional and unintentional harms every day at work. This is layered upon the societal racism and sexism that women of color endure (and particularly Black women, due to the deep anti-Blackness in the U.S.). The harm caused by this unrelenting emotional labor is multilayered, intersecting, and cumulative, and *it is killing us.*

The System Will Not Be Complicit in Its Own Demise

"The grounding for changing workplace culture, in my view, has to start with a challenge to the white dominant culture norm of productivity/capitalism above all else—I don't believe you can work on equity/inclusion if the organization is not willing to radically change the paradigm of squeezing every productive minute out of exhausted employees."

—Multiracial philanthropic leader survey participant

We must seriously question the application of profit-driven approaches to our nonprofit and community-serving workplaces. Workplaces, particularly those that serve and represent our communities, should be where we first, and above all else, commit to do no harm and to invest in our collective, interdependent, and sustained well-being. Exploiting the people we task with serving and representing our communities is a dangerous incongruence that reflects our lack of values alignment in organizational cultures, structures, and leadership approaches.

I can't tell you how often I've had to counter the pro-capitalist/pro-business mindset in not-for-profit work settings. Most of those times, I was dismissed as naïve, foolish, or resentful. The underlying beliefs and assumptions of this business-knows-best dogma are alive and kicking in philanthropy, nonprofits, boardrooms, and supposedly progressive nonprofit leadership. We see it show up in businessmen (still predominantly male) who champion profit as a sound policy framework, wealth as wisdom, and return on investment as equivalent to community well-being. We see it in nonprofits recruiting individuals with business success as a promise for nonprofit missions being realized. We see this in the nonprofit world adopting business models, business plans, and strategic plans (business and strategic plans have their origins in the military, so layer that on!) and using business terminology, mental models, and strategies—as if everything could be reduced to quantification, optimization, maximization of cost-savings, and the efficient social production of widget-makers through standardized and rote education practices.

We see this in human resources practices that fail to consider the complexity of humans and human interaction, and in organizational models that fail to provide workers with pay and benefits that consider their dignity and long-term well-being. As Vu Le reminds us in "No, Social Enterprise and Earned Revenues Will Not Solve Nonprofits' Funding Problems":

> Most for-profit businesses fail after a few years: According to the U.S. Bureau of Labor Statistics, approximately 20% of new businesses fail during the first two years of operation, and about 45% fail during the first five years. This statistic is based on data collected from 1994 to 2020, before the Plague. Another study found that the failure rate for new businesses was around 50% after five years and around 70% after ten years. And these are for-profit entities that can just focus on making money and don't have to simultaneously deal with running nonprofit programs and services.[1]

> *"It took me a while to see what we were doing [at work]. We were doing work around financial literacy, which meant that if you're leaving a domestic violence situation, you need to make sure you have money to take care of yourself and manage it. But, for the staff working there, they didn't pay us enough for us to leave our partner if we were in an abusive situation, right? So it's things like that, realizing that it's really the nonprofit industrial complex in general that helps keep things as they are."*

> —KRISTA, Black nonprofit leader

The fact that our workplaces and leadership models center competition, perfectionism, and binary and zero-sum thinking is not accidental or isolated. This business-knows-best philosophy is close kin with imperialism and colonialism; it is individualistic, competitive, arrogant, and supremacist. From a community-first perspective, it is also irrational and inhumane. In fact, as someone who grew up in what is referred to as the *developing world* (or, more judgmentally, the *third world*), I recognize the bridge between current mainstream workplace cultures and global supremacist machinations: the imposition of neoliberal policies, such as structural adjustment, forced privatization, deregulation, and the abdication of solidarity approaches. What feels to some in the U.S. like abstract political dialogue and bumper-sticker ideology has had very real and harmful effects in my birth country and many other countries of the Global South.

Alicia, a Latine nonprofit leader, described her experience of working in nonprofit organizations as an immigrant woman of color as going through what felt like "domestication"—being conditioned to accept dominant-culture ways of seeing the world and having her behaviors, her voice, and her values silenced and corrected. In her work, Alicia refused to center donors, boards, or even herself as the organization's executive leader. Instead, she described her leadership as *"only a whisper of what the community is."*

In her article "Building Prisms of the People within the Nonprofit Industrial Complex," Michelle Oyakawa asserts, "The idea that organizational leaders should be accountable primarily to their [community] members rather than to grantmakers' or other elites' priorities runs counter to much contemporary practice. Nonprofit organizations are often more accountable to wealthy donors than they are to the constituencies they advocate for or claim to represent."[2] To shift away from this dominant practice and turn toward each other and engage with the collective nature of social change work, Oyakawa writes, we need to build *people power*, which

> would mean funders giving up control over organizations' agendas and allowing groups to direct their activities, rather than being guided by

funders' strategic plans. It would mean giving people the resources to build relationships with each other without onerous expectations about "deliverables" designed to meet funders' goals. Investing in people power would entail allocating resources to leaders who have built trust and will be accountable to people in their community, rather than basing funding decisions primarily on who writes the best grant applications.[3]

About a third of the women interviewed talked about workplace culture using terms from intimate violence relationships. In describing what it was like to work in mainstream nonprofit organizations with an abusive white woman as her boss, Rosario, a Latine nonprofit leader, said: *"And everything just like a perpetrator, right?"*

All of this is to say that the ideas upon which our workplaces are built are rooted in social, political, philosophical, and religious beliefs that have violently shaped our world for centuries—they are not magically isolated from the ideas that have shaped societies for decades. So we must start by acknowledging that we cannot change our workplaces or our leaders unless, as Hildy Gottlieb explains in her article "How Nonprofits Can Truly Advance Change,"[4] we change the assumptions underlying our institutions, our policies, and our power dynamics; and unless we change ourselves.

The system will not be complicit in its own demise. It is built to endure, to replicate itself, and to squelch dissent. In the following chapters, we'll explore the context in which the stories shared in this book took place. Understanding the context will help us move toward creating a new type of workplace, one that is fully informed and aware of where we are and where we've come from.

CHAPTER 15

Understanding and Recreating the Container

The workplace

"Whenever you're invited someplace, it's . . . not just as a leader . . . It's always the hyphenated identity leader; it's never being fully accepted."

—LUCIA, Latine educational leader

Understanding the context within which this book's stories take place is critical to more fully grasp what a significant uphill battle, at times a Sisyphean endeavor, it is for women of color to make it to leadership positions. In this chapter, I share some notable aspects of philanthropic and nonprofit workplaces as relevant to the leadership and experiences of women of color.

Women of Color in Philanthropy

"I think, given the experience we've had getting to where we are (in our leadership), we do see the world differently and have ideas that could be different and effective. And when I look at trust-based philanthropy, it is not coincidental that most of those who are engaged in practicing it are BIPOC women."

—SOLEDAD, Latine philanthropic leader

Within the philanthropic sector, the statistics across race and gender lines are worth reviewing. As I've stated earlier in the book, institutional philanthropy as a sector has an outsized influence. While the total dollars that philanthropy wields is a fraction of what government funding represents, philanthropy has a tremendous influence on nonprofits and how they conduct their work (even what they focus on at work), influences policy and policy-makers, and too often makes or breaks nascent nonprofits and community-led efforts dependent on grant funding. Philanthropy has a history of co-opting and diluting movements through monetary influence and control. Given this outsized influence, it is crucial to understand who leads and shapes the culture of philanthropy. From the 2020 Council on Foundations annual survey:[1]

- A majority (76.5%) of full-time staff in philanthropic organizations identify as female (*foundation workforce is not representative of the total population; women and white people are overrepresented*)

- Over half (57.8%) of foundation CEOs identify as female (*female-dominated and well-paid: unusual!*)

- Nearly 90% of administrative foundation staff identify as female.

- A majority of foundation staff identify as white (72.7%); 11.3% identify as Black; 6.9% identify as "Hispanic"; 5.2% Asian; 0.06% American Indian/Alaska Native; 0.04% Pacific Islander/Hawaiian; 0.04% Middle Eastern or North African; and 1.9% biracial or multiracial.

- About 90% (89.7%) of all foundation CEOs are white. *Let me say that again*: In a country that is 12% Black, 18.5% Latinx, 5.6% Asian, 0.7% Indigenous (*we should be horrified that the Indigenous population of this land stands at under 1% of the total population*), 2.8% multiracial, *9 out of 10 foundation CEOs are white.*

- 64% of foundation administrative staff are white, and about one-third of administrative foundation staff identify as people of color.

Notice the dramatic disparity between staff of color and leadership of color. Given the profoundly hierarchical nature of the philanthropic structure and culture, *it matters that people of color are so much more represented in administrative than leadership roles*. It matters for the perspectives, experiences, sensibilities, and voices that are brought in to determine the path ahead, shaping what is valued. It matters when you consider that women (especially women of color) advocate for their teams, work for staff well-being and work/life balance, and work for equity, inclusion, and diversity at higher rates than men or white women. *Who leads matters to how we lead, and how we lead shapes our culture.*

- Less than 2% (1.6%) of foundation CEOs are Latine; this includes male and female, U.S.-born and foreign-born. I represent one of under 2% of foundation CEOs in the U.S. who are foreign-born immigrant Latinx women. The experiences and perspectives I bring with my leadership are far from the norm in philanthropy. While there are myriad reasons for this disproportionally low representation of Latine in top philanthropic leadership, a 2022 article in *Hispanic Executive* cites workplaces that don't value diversity, limited opportunities for advancement within the dominant culture, and misalignment with one's values and vision as top reasons why Latinas are leaving their workplaces.[2] In other words, there is a lack of and need for psychological safety in our workplaces. The fact that Latinas make, on average, 57 cents for every dollar a white man makes should also be considered.

Monetizing What's Valued

"Just different treatment . . . not being paid the same."

—ANGELA, Black nonprofit leader

What about compensation in a country where money is supreme and everything has a price tag? How do the salaries of white male CEOs compare to those of white women, Black women, Latinx women, Asian American women, Indigenous women, and trans women? A 2019 Council on Foundations annual salary survey found that a gender gap in salaries persists, with women CEOs making about 83 cents for every dollar a male CEO makes.[3] As mentioned, Latinas in the U.S. earn 57 cents to every dollar that a white man earns. As a Latine woman foundation CEO, that doesn't sit right with me. Women of color's hard work translates into significantly less financial security and intergenerational wealth than that of white men and white women doing similar work. This inequity is exacerbated by the fact that women of color carry out additional dimensions of culture work that are not expected of white leaders, so *we're paid less and expected to do more.*

For example, I am aware that as a foundation CEO I made approximately 60 percent of the annual salary that the white male leaders (my former bosses) made, even though those men led foundations significantly smaller in endowment size and with similar or smaller staff size (both standard measures used to calibrate salary). I am also aware that one man's starting salary was significantly higher than the woman CEO he replaced, even though he had considerably less relevant experience. These jobs were our first as foundation CEO for both men and myself. Considering that their salary level was from many years earlier and in geographies with a significantly lower cost of living, the gap between their compensation and mine was likely even more significant.

As one of the few Latina foundation CEOs in the U.S., I face these realities, which are a problem for me and my family. They are a problem for all women of color, and for society as a whole if we endeavor to repair the profound harm that racism and sexism cause and close the abysmal racial and gender wealth gaps.

As Shanti, an Asian American nonprofit leader, said, *"I think that the systems are built for white people, and therefore anything that challenges that or is different makes people uncomfortable; and that translates into unclear communication and assumptions, and perhaps that leads to just different treatment, you know, which often comes in the form of, for example, not being paid the same way."*

These realities additionally contribute to what Edgar Villanueva has referred to as the *racial philanthropy gap*, where white leaders disproportionately control the wealth held by philanthropy. A look at current grantmaking practices indicates that overrepresentation of white leadership in philanthropy profoundly impacts where philanthropic wealth is directed: less than 9% of total grantmaking is going to communities of color, including a paltry 0.4% to Indigenous communities, 0.6% for Latinx communities, and 1.8% in Black communities.[4] More specifically, organizations with leaders of color are significantly less likely to receive funding (and they receive less when they are funded) than comparable organizations with white leaders.

Women of Color in Nonprofits

The income gap is even wider in non-foundation nonprofits: women CEOs at these nonprofits make 75% of what male CEOs make, according to Candid's *2020 Nonprofit Compensation* report.[5] Women of color working in nonprofits are likelier to report being underpaid and, along with white women, are most likely to earn under $50,000 per year and least likely to make over $100,000 per year, as reported in the *Chronicle of Philanthropy*.[6]

A fascinating study by the Building Movement Project and funded by the Robert Sterling Clark Foundation, *Making or Taking Space*, shares findings that resonate at such a deep level for me that I was ecstatic when I learned a more extensive study of this sort was conducted, *Trading Glass Ceilings for Glass Cliffs*.[7] Among the key findings of these studies:

- The intention to hire a leader of color following the tenure of a white leader commonly coincided with internal challenges around race and racism.

- The extent of internal troubles was often not known by incoming leaders of color, who were still expected to resolve long-standing issues.

- Incoming leaders of color were expected to take on both the executive leadership responsibilities and racial equity work and healing racial tensions.

- Few organizations viewed this additional labor of racial equity and addressing long-standing race-related tensions as meriting additional compensation, even though it is an additional stream of work, needs a different set of skills, and requires deep emotional labor (*I invite you to read this again while recalling the statistics on racial and gender pay gaps*).

- Leaders of color invited to bring about culture change faced significant challenges and resistance to change from the very people who hired them (board and staff).

Behind these statistics about women of color leaders are *human beings* with lives outside work, with social and emotional realities, living in a country with deep racial and gender disparities across all measures of society and rampant racist violence. While the U.S. population becomes more diverse, white Americans continue to live in predominantly white spaces and have predominantly white social networks.[8] Because Americans have highly racialized social networks, people of color find themselves in majority-white workplaces but still outside the social network of their colleagues and managers, even as workplaces become more intentional about diversity.[9]

> *"My appearance and performance has to be flawless at all times when white colleagues often show up unprepared. I'm often the only WOC in 'powerful leadership' spaces. My ideas, reflections, and thoughts are often stolen by white colleagues and presented as their own."*
>
> —Black nonprofit leader survey participant

In majority-white workplaces, this often means being the only, the first, or one of the few women of color in a social context where most people you work with not only have certain cultural commonalities but are more likely to belong to the same social networks.

For women of color in fields where they are an extreme minority, their sense of belonging and safety, peer support, and mentorship are profoundly impacted. As mentioned earlier in this book, the women leaders I interviewed named the lack of mentorship opportunities for women of color (specifically mentorship tailored for women of color and/or with women of color as mentors) a significant barrier and challenge in their careers. Every single woman of color I spoke to mentioned the importance and need for spaces to connect with and mutually support other women of color:

"Because you and I know that every time women of color get together, the conversations turn to the shit we have to put up with."

—KRISTA, Black nonprofit leader

This reality, and the fact that humans are innately social animals, is another reason why efforts to diversify without working on inclusion and belonging at the cultural level are not just incomplete but harmful.

And because these dynamics are rooted in broader cultural norms, the troubling statistics and stories are not limited to the philanthropic or nonprofit worlds. The largest study about the state of women in corporate America, the *Women in the Workplace* report from McKinsey and LeanIn.Org, points to a consistency in the experiences of women of color across all workplaces and underlines the need for wholesale systems- and structural-level changes to how we organize ourselves and how we think about and nurture leadership:

- Women represent 28% of C-suite corporate leadership positions; and women of color represent only 6% of C-suite positions.

- Women of color experience burnout and microaggressions and carry emotional labor and advocacy for DEI efforts disproportionately more than men or white women.

- Women of color in corporate workplaces have less access to support systems, self-care, and recognition for their contributions.[10]

Quoting from the *Women in the Workplace 2023* report referenced earlier:

> Years of data show that women experience microaggressions at a significantly higher rate than men: they are twice as likely to be mistaken for someone junior and hear comments on their emotional state. For women with traditionally marginalized identities, these slights happen more often and are even more demeaning. As just one example, Asian and Black women are seven times more likely than white women to be confused with someone of the same race and ethnicity.[11]

Social Context

The COVID-19 pandemic made some of these injustices more visible, and it also worsened workplace conditions, particularly for BIPOC communities, contributing to what many referred to as the Great Resignation.[12] For a thorough snapshot analysis of the situation for BIPOC in the workplace during COVID-19, you should read Hue's report *Unsafe. Unheard. Unvalued. A State of Inequity.*[13] The Hue report notes a disproportionate burden and impact on women of color in the workplace.

As if all of this weren't enough, a 2020 study of fundraisers found that three out of four fundraisers have experienced sexual harassment and that "fundraisers of color and fundraisers who were lesbian, bisexual, or gay said they were sexually coerced at work at higher rates than white and heterosexual fundraisers."[14]

> *"Invisible when accomplishing work with excellence, visible when being gaslighted; having to explain experiences/real life over and over in white spaces; feeling isolated and alone; lack of mentors who share my experience."*
>
> —Black nonprofit leader survey participant

As we consider the context in which women of color leaders work and live, let's complete the picture by taking into account the endless ways that U.S. society disproportionately harms women of color in myriad aspects of their life:

- The compelling research on weathering, which finds that repeated exposure to racism and other adverse social conditions causes premature aging and related health risks, speaks to the deep toll interpersonal and structural racism take on (especially Black) women of color at the cellular level and on populations as a whole;[15]

- layer on epigenetics and intergenerational and historical trauma and their impact on physical and mental health and life expectancy;[16]

- the horrific racial disparities in maternal mortality that claim so many Black mothers' lives;[17]

- wealth gaps that maintain the unjust status quo generation after generation;[18]

- racialized and classist incarceration rates that maintain the legacy of slavery through state-sanctioned imprisonment and criminalization of those living in poverty;[19]

- deep disparities in homeownership that deny communities of color the intergenerational wealth that property has provided white families;[20]

- racialized police brutality that disproportionately harms and murders Black and Brown communities;[21]

- murdered and missing Indigenous women, whose cases go unsolved, unprosecuted, and too frequently not even investigated;[22]

- unlivable wages and racial wage gaps that work to maintain the status quo;[23]

- the frayed and fragmented safety net that shifts the responsibility for systemic problems created over decades and centuries from the state to individuals (and nonprofits);

and the inevitable conclusion is that *the comfort of the status quo is killing us*.

We live in a world of mutually reinforcing unjust systems, and these systems' relentlessness hums us to indifference, helplessness, hopelessness, unhealthiness, self-harming behaviors and thoughts, and to undervaluing ourselves and each other. *All injustices are interconnected.* This results in what Elizabeth Castillo describes in her article calling for a change in management styles at workplaces:

> A business mindset often rationalizes inhumane labor practices like paying sub-living wages, not providing healthcare insurance or paid time off, and limiting employee autonomy through command-and-control leadership. People of color and women are disproportionately affected by these practices. For example, 20 percent of workers report feeling disrespected at work; the rate increases to 33 percent for Black workers. Supervisors, managers, and senior leaders often perpetuate racial inequity in the workplace. Dehumanization also shows up when organizations tolerate bullying, toxic leadership, and power abuses.[24]

CHAPTER 16

Containers of Culture

Dismantling supremacist scaffolding

*What happens in our interpersonal relationships is
mirrored and reinforced by the larger systems.*

—MARIAME KABA, *We Do This 'Til We Free Us*

Most organizations don't consciously or intentionally adopt or espouse
white supremacist values or beliefs. Most organizations would be quite
horrified at the suggestion that they, in any way, embody white supremacy. As Yonason Goldson states, "Every choice you make contributes to a
new cultural norm. Your actions combine with similar choices of others;
they also legitimize similar choices by others."[1] Because white supremacy
is in the DNA of U.S. culture, it lives unbothered in all institutions and
systems unless intentional and sustained culture change makes it visible
and works to replace it with a values-driven anti-racist culture that is nurtured, adapted, and actively maintained.

This is an essential discernment: *white supremacy will continue to
thrive and reproduce without anyone tending to it*. If we do nothing, the
ubiquity and impact of white supremacy in workplaces will continue,
regardless of the good intentions of the people working there. To disrupt and eventually deconstruct and replace white supremacy requires a
great deal of intention: unrelenting, collective, and ever-adaptive intentional efforts.

Indeed, as Gail Christopher and Deepa Iyer state, "Today, organizations and society have an unprecedented opportunity to honor and support the leadership of women of color and to transform the culture and systems within which all Americans live."[2]

We keep making organizations in the same mold: unquestioned power distribution and supremacist values. Even in organizations purportedly committed to social justice, we keep borrowing the oppressor's tools and defining success according to often irrelevant and ungrounded metrics selected by individuals and organizations external to the issues or people affected by the issues being addressed. In order to change our workplaces, we must understand that our organizational structures and cultures are products of centuries of colonizing worldviews, consumed with (male) hero and messianic leaders, individualistic competition, and material accumulation. Acknowledging the genocidal origins of the U.S. is, therefore, a necessary step in truly changing our workplace cultures.

Let's be clear: the stories shared in this book and the behaviors women of color experienced in multiple workspaces were abusive, and these behaviors were buoyed in the work culture by

- rampant gaslighting
- tactical manipulation of workplace relationships
- withholding acknowledgment and taking credit for work done by women of color
- distorting the truth and telling lies
- creating tensions among coworkers (divide and conquer)
- exclusion from decision-making, from meetings, from opportunity
- setting unrealistic expectations and deadlines
- activating golden handcuffs (when previously "compliant" employees begin to awake to the abuse)
- withholding necessary support and resources

In short, well-known traits of abusive relationships, settler-colonialism, and intimate partner violence. This observation of organizational cultures mirroring abusive relationships is not a coincidence or a paranoid delusion; it is the reasonable and predictable effect of the ideas that shape this country and the structures or arrangements that have been developed to contain those ideas. Our institutions, structures, and practices are the offspring of the cultural beliefs and values that founded this nation. The founding of this nation is inextricably tied to and built upon the enslavement of Black human beings who were violently taken from their homes to another continent for the purpose of exploitation and violence under the moral authority of Christian institutions and the genocide of Indigenous communities across the vast land that is now the United States.

Fortunately, structures can be changed, and once changed, new structures can produce new effects, which in turn can change ideas, which can then iteratively shape structures, and so on. Later in this book, we'll explore how ideas, structures, and effects play together in workplaces.

In the workplaces where I experienced abusive behaviors, I was never the only person who experienced abuse, because just like in abusive relationships, there is a high likelihood that someone who is abusive to one partner will be abusive to future partners. I was never the sole target of abuse because it was *not about me*—it was about the culture, the power dynamics, and ultimately, the ideas that underlaid the structures and cultures of the organizations. Workplace abuse is very gendered, targeting women (including trans women), and it is highly racialized, an idea deep at the core of U.S. society. In this context, women of color are concurrently experiencing (and trying to heal from) racialized and gendered abuse in the workplace and in society. *This is draining us.*

Workplace abuse harms people of color disproportionately (but certainly not exclusively), and as shared in the stories from my and other women of color's experiences, people of color with power can also play key roles in upholding supremacist power dynamics that they benefited from. Supremacy is nuanced and survives and thrives by recruiting a diversity of people to its service. *Even supremacy recognizes the strength of a diverse group.*

White supremacy is a key ingredient in U.S. culture, and culture is transmitted and protected by the structures we create. To create anti-racist cultures, we must work on (i.e., meaningfully change) the structures within and between our workplaces. The existing dominant cultural models conspire to keep us stuck in supremacist frameworks. Challenges and discomfort are met with confirmation bias: it doesn't feel good, so it must be wrong; it feels unfamiliar, so it must be harmful. What has worked in the past is assumed to be a universal truth, without interrogating how what "worked" was evaluated or with whose "metrics." Given the vast racial and gender disparities in the U.S., existing dominant models have only worked for a portion of the population and not at all for collective well-being, for our social and natural ecosystems, or for our basic humanity.

CHAPTER 17

Inspecting the Scaffolding

The idea that structures contain and shape culture is not new and is beautifully explained in the piece by Design Studio for Social Intervention, "Ideas Arrangements Effects: Systems Design and Social Justice." The simple yet profound concept in the article is that "ideas are embedded within social arrangements, which in turn produce effects."[1] *Yes!* Our organizations' structures, processes, and interactions are produced, held, transmitted, and enhanced by a white-dominant culture that has been created and fortified over hundreds of years. As I have said at work ad nauseam, work structures are containers of culture, and as such, they are shaped by, transmit, and reinforce values, beliefs, and power dynamics.

The ideas, assumptions, and beliefs that are the scaffolding of our dominant culture and institutions have been transmitted through generations, becoming invisible through their omnipresence and leading us to believe they are natural and inevitable. How often do we hear at institutions "That's just the way it is," or the even more insidious "That's how it's always been done"? Many women leaders I interviewed named this a common barrier to their work, particularly efforts at workplace transformation. As Diya, a South Asian American educational leader, said, *"There is still a lot of resistance to what I bring. I often hear, 'Well, we don't do things that way around here.' In theory, organizations want to hire people with different points of view, but when it comes down to changing the operations, they just can't entertain it."*

As the "Ideas Arrangements Effects" article states, "Big ideas remain sturdy because of how they embed themselves in everyday life."[2] From the deeply American obsession with productivity,[3] to the unquestioned belief that competition ushers the best outcomes, to the individualistic (versus collectivist) focus of U.S. culture, these ideas are built into our institutions' and systems' structures (arrangements). As we have seen, even ideas that seem innocuous, like professionalism, expose their racist roots when examined.

Professionalism was a concept mentioned by most of the women leaders I interviewed, and particularly talked about by the Black women leaders, who spoke of their many experiences of comments, behaviors, and expectations regarding their natural hair and hair wraps in the context of professional appearance. And because professionalism seems race-neutral at first, some women talked about their journey in recognizing that professionalism is a racialized concept:

> *"But for me, I was raised as a Black woman. I must be twice as good and work twice as hard as everybody else. So, professionalism means I'm aspiring to the white-supremacist standard. In the process, I am an instrument of white supremacy because now I'm judging other people based on what professionalism is viewed to be... and then I have had to evaluate this concept of professionalism because it's a myth. It's fabricated."*

> —DANIELLE, Black nonprofit leader

In the same way, white-dominant culture manifests in our workplaces through its perfectionism, sense of urgency, defensiveness, illusion of objectivity, individualism, belief in "one right way," binary thinking, concentrated power, paternalism, right to comfort, conflict avoidance, and other ideas that go unnoticed by most members of the dominant culture.[4]

As these ideas (white-supremacist culture) are built into the structures and processes of institutions and workplaces (arrangements), they have predictable outcomes (effects), such as disproportionate white leadership in workplaces and boards, and gender and racial pay gaps dramatically favoring men and white people. Overall, labor in the U.S. is exploitative;

labor protections are written for the benefit of the wealth accumulators, not for workers, not for humanity in general or the planet. These are predictable outcomes (effects) when you start with a collection of ideas that includes white supremacy, patriarchy, Christianity, anthropocentrism, unfettered free-market commodification, and colonization. Built on a foundation of such ideas, work in the U.S., regardless of sector, is unsurprisingly out of balance and particularly inhospitable for women of color.

> *"It's the unconscious bias of others that's hardest to deal with.*
> *Like when I go to a lecture hall to speak and someone hands me the*
> *trash to take out—that's a person who doesn't conceive of a Black or*
> *Brown person as the speaker, they must be the help."*

> —Multiracial survey participant

The article by Design Studio for Social Intervention points out that the relationship between ideas, arrangements, and effects is not linear or mono-directional, nor monogamous. Multiple arrangements can and do overlap (think *intersectionality*[5]), and effects can lead to new arrangements, which may mutate an underlying idea into new arrangements, birthing new effects. So while organizational culture may present as invisible, it is nonetheless very complex, dynamic, and mutable.

Despite growing investments in diversity, equity, and inclusion (DEI) programming, we have not and will not change our workspaces through one-time DEI workshops or any approach focusing only on the *effects* or *outcomes*. As Lily Zheng has made clear in her book *DEI Deconstructed*, we must reframe DEI as a collective effort toward fairness and justice in our workplaces.[6] Sustainable DEI efforts must go beyond reactionary or sporadic trainings, and they must engage accountability across all levels of the organization, particularly leadership.

Developing a strategic plan stating that we will work toward justice is not-enough to undo the supremacist ideas developed and refined over centuries and inherent in our dominant work arrangements, which exploit and produce unequal and unfair experiences, burnout, and harm. And as laid out in the article "Process and Practice: Linking Organizational Strategy and Race Equity Work," we must understand that working toward racial equity and justice *is* a strategic plan![7] If your strategy is not rooted in your values, and your values aren't the building blocks of equity work, then your strategy will not undo the deeply seated white supremacy and colonized mindsets inherent in our institutions. Racial equity work that happens separate from a strategic plan devoid of anti-racism work is not just very likely to fail, it is likely to cause harm, especially to BIPOC staff and communities.

We must question *everything*. We must experiment and be willing to be uncomfortable while working with the unfamiliar. The way forward will emerge and be emergent, and it will be fueled by curiosity, diversity of thought (imagination), and commitment to a practice based on explicitly and collectively named and explored values.

Let's take, for example, an unquestioned element of organizational structure: supervisors and managers. As noted in Caitlin Rosenthal's research, the supervisory function in the modern workplace can be understood through its oppressive and exploitative origin: "Modern business management practices employed by corporations and nonprofits—creating middle managers, performance management, productivity analysis, and workforce planning—can all be traced back to the management of plantation slavery," Rosenthal writes.[8]

How many of us know that modern U.S. management practices are rooted in slavery? If, like me, you have not seen the explicit connection between the two, we should ask ourselves: Why are the origins of modern U.S. workplace management in slavery not shared more openly? There are extensive publications on the matter, so it isn't from lack of existing knowledge and evidence. The "norm" of supervisory management practices is a great illustration of how the ideas behind workplace arrangements become invisible, which leads us to ignore the values and assumptions inherent in our workplace structures.

It shouldn't be surprising, then, that women of color leaders are often the catalysts for structural changes in workplaces. Many women I spoke to referenced approaching workplace structure and hierarchy differently. As Rosario, a Latine nonprofit leader, shared, *"And it's about how we distribute power. For us, one way we are trying to dismantle the hierarchy is that all the jobs, tasks, and tools are at the same level of importance."*

Identifying and making visible the ideas behind supervision can help us create new structures in our workplaces based on different ideas that value, support, and nurture the people in our organizations. Because, as Kim-Monique Johnson states in "How to Be an Antiracist Supervisor: Start with Changing What You Call Yourself," "pushing staff to work harder, longer, and with fewer resources is toxic for staff and costly for nonprofit organizations in more ways than one."[9]

Using this framework for identifying the ideas behind our arrangements is one key way to change the effects of our workplaces (on workers and communities) by naming and exploring the implicit assumptions and cultural forces that undergird the organizational structure. Starting from a place of explicitly shared values, we can co-create new worker relationships and structures that manifest a commitment to care, solidarity, and overall well-being, rather than unquestioningly replicating or building upon a supervision model rooted in slavery.

For every woman I spoke to, changing the status quo was an essential part of what made their leadership different from mainstream, traditional notions of leadership. Lucia, a Latine educational leader, said, *"Embodying power means a challenge to traditional power; it means being able to think of how you can use your talents and your skills to challenge the status quo and to move things in a different direction, in ways that are not necessarily acknowledged."*

The recognition that workplaces carry in them implicit values and beliefs is also explored in an enlightening way in Frederic Laloux's *Reinventing Organizations* (and I am grateful to a former board chair and current friend for sharing Laloux's work with me).[10] In Laloux's thinking,

"Organizations as we know them today are simply the expression of our current worldview, our current stage of development. Every time that we, as a species, have changed the way we think about the world, we have come up with more powerful types of organizations."[11] Laloux proposes various types of organizations (named after colors) and their underlying values and beliefs. While organizations primarily feature the values of one organizational type and stage, it is important to note that organizations generally contain a mix of archetypes.

Laloux's work, based on extensive cross-national organizational research, strongly supports the need to diversify organizational leadership, finding that the values and worldviews of the leader(s) most strongly determine the type of organization and culture adopted. If leaders disproportionately influence organizational culture, then we need to intentionally co-create spaces that support, nourish, and elevate the leadership of women of color, which is essential to our dreams of liberatory spaces and just workplaces (as part of a full overhaul of white supremacy and patriarchal culture). Given that all the women I interviewed talked about the centrality of community and working for what is best for the community— not for themselves or their organization—imagine what could happen to our society and world if more organizational leaders put the collective good above personal or partisan gain.

"I now understand power to be the unspoken currency that I can leverage to accomplish the goal . . . that's in the best interest of the collective."

—DANIELLE, Black nonprofit leader

Applying lessons from Laloux and the "Ideas Arrangements Effects" article, it becomes apparent that if we keep propping up the same types of leaders, we will continue to produce the same types of organizations and workplaces (and their impacts on our communities). Further, if we expect and demand that women of color, despite their own experiences, perspectives, and values, sustain the same types of organizations and organizational cultures as white leaders have created for decades, we are shutting down essential pathways to new ways of working together, new ways to shape institutions and organizations, while also harming the people who are putting themselves on the line to make a new way possible.

A basic but essential step of this work is making the status quo visible to those who experience it as "natural" and right. Making the current toxic status quo visible must include people understanding that healthier, more just, and inclusive workplaces will benefit *all* workers, including workers who identify as white, male, and Christian.

Let me be clear: I am not proposing that there should not be white leaders anymore. I assert that our institutions, which contain our workplaces, have historically been fed on a robust diet of white supremacy, patriarchy, competition, perfectionism, hyper-individualism, and other white-dominant culture traits. I assert that the further someone is from a white, cis-male, Christian identity, the more challenging it is to make it up the well-worn grooves to leadership. I assert that the effects of white supremacy and patriarchy have been harmful to our society and all people, including those holding unearned privileges and power. By being intentional about creating cultures that don't just tolerate but nurture leaders with wide-ranging identities and experiences, our organizations (and the way we work) will change to welcome and produce outcomes that are suited for individuals and communities beyond, yet inclusive of the presumptive white, male gaze inherent in our workplace cultures.

> *"A place where people don't look at me as a diverse hire,*
> *but as a qualified professional."*
>
> —Latine nonprofit leader survey participant

Boards

Legally, boards are integral elements of nonprofit organizations. Every woman I spoke to named boards as a source of harm in their professional life. Many of the challenges leaders of color face in leading organizational culture change are related to navigating the thorny power dynamics of nonprofit boards. For example, a survey conducted by the Trust-Based Philanthropy Project found that philanthropic boards' resistance to shifting toward trust-based approaches was the number one barrier named by survey participants.[12] (Because of philanthropy's outsized influence on the nonprofit sector, this philanthropic resistance to more power-aware approaches affects workers in nonprofits too.) It is of note that the trust-based philanthropy (TBP) approach, at its core, is about identifying and shifting power dynamics within and among philanthropic and nonprofit entities. As a side note, as someone who practices TBP approaches and is very familiar with the work of the TBP Project, I would argue that TBP, when combined with a real commitment to racial equity, is currently the most viable framework for advancing effective and racially just philanthropy.

An excellent resource for boards preparing for leadership transition to a leader of color is a report by the Building Movement Project and BoardSource, *Avoiding the Glass Cliff: Advice to Boards on Preparing for and Supporting a New Leader of Color.*[13] Personally, this resource gave credence to my personal experience and repeated frustration with the way boards treated (harmed) me and other women of color leaders. The findings of this report, as well as related reports by the Building Movement Project, were a salve to the unrelenting gaslighting, mistreatment, and microaggressions that I have experienced as a leader. Hopefully, by having research and recommendations addressing systemic issues, individuals serving on boards can approach preparation for transitioning to and supporting leaders of color in a constructive and open-minded way rather than rooted in defensive, reactionary, and shame-avoidant ways. Highlighting particularly salient findings and recommendations from this report:

- Define and invest in racial equity in your organization's culture (board and staff), operations, and succession planning.

- Honestly address board composition, dysfunction (particularly around power dynamics), and areas where the board has learning and growing to do.

- Work with search partners who have experience and an explicit plan for recruiting leaders of color, which should include guiding the board in preparation for supporting a new leader of color.

- Be self-aware and honest about the organization's current state with finalists for the position.

- Consider a compensation package that addresses the specific circumstances of leaders of color, and do not assume that compensation approaches should be colorblind.

- Be real about the current racial and gender dynamics (and the dynamic of those intersecting dimensions) in your organization. Be honest with this information if you expect the new leader to be responsible for developing organizational racial equity and the necessary culture change.

- Do the work of thinking through what might be different for the board, staff, and new leader when they support leadership styles that differ from traditional, male, white, and Christian leadership approaches.

CHAPTER 18

Leading for Survival, Leading for Liberation

"Ultimately, the challenge is transforming individual organizations and society by developing equitable systems, practices, and institutions."

—GAIL CHRISTOPHER AND DEEPA IYER,
"Honoring and Supporting Women of Color Leaders"

It is not just our workplace cultures that are shaped by white supremacy; the very way we *think about work* in our lives is a result of capitalism, which is intimately tied to racist systems of exploitation, extraction, and racial violence. My dear friend and amazing community leader Karina Barillas says, "We've been taught that you have to produce and that your work is a reflection of your worth."[1] Capitalism has made work central to our lives and identities, and the economic and social arrangements in the U.S. enforce the belief of work as life. Creating new, liberating configurations of work should change workplace cultures and the very conception of work and its place in our lives.

An article by Faima Bakar, "There's No Such Thing As a Dream Job, No One Aspires to Do Labour," is a good (and sadly necessary) reminder that there is more to life than our jobs. Bakar posits that "really, our work should be a complementary part of our lives—something that has a purpose, allows us to use problem-solving skills, make connections—but that doesn't bulldoze over everything else."[2] Tish Harrison Warren further explores this point in her piece "How to Fight Back against the Inhumanity of Modern Work," where she explores the impact of digital technology (including productivity monitoring) and a productivity-obsessed culture—it is the human soul, trust, and human connection that are sacrificed when our lives are out of balance due to work.[3]

My brother recently sent me and my sister the article "The Wages of Overwork" by Anne Helen Petersen. The reality is all three of us have struggled with overwork while understanding that it is not healthy, not aligned with our values, and not natural—yet we've been stuck in overwork, to varying degrees, for years. The article indicates that workers with higher incomes and graduate degrees are more likely to perform work outside of work hours. That finding should be considered alongside the finding that as women of color rise in leadership and responsibility at work, "the intersectional threats posed by patterns of misogyny and racism intensify, rather than lessen," compounding the pressures that women of color leaders face.[4]

Capitalist values have created conditions such that, as Petersen says,

> the norms of the rich and powerful influence the norms of those striving to be rich and powerful. Work culture at the highest echelons, in the most handsomely-paid professions, trickles down to professions where work is far more precarious. Today, people with paid time off (which, generally, are also people who are not lower income) work more hours and, when they have paid time off, don't take the full amount. Not because they love their work, but because that's the standard—and they've rationalized that they don't need it.[5]

These attitudes contribute to a cultural belief that working more is morally good and diminish empathy for work conditions faced by lower-income workers, as higher-income earners set "overwork" as an aspiration. Further, Petersen states, "the less money you make, the more likely you are to not have enough work . . . 23% of lower-income workers report that they have too few working hours, compared to 4% of upper-income workers."[6] Given this reality, and that the proportion of people working multiple jobs has increased in the past couple of decades, low-income earners and women are more likely to work multiple jobs.[7]

Amid all this overwork, when do we have time to build community? To care for our families, our friends, our neighbors? When do we have time to care for ourselves? How can we value and prioritize imagination, play, joy, and other essential practices for radical change, when working to exhaustion is held up as exemplar?

Burnout

"A culture of rest, where we are not expected to be constantly available, or acting from a place of urgency (which is part of white supremacy culture)."

—Latine nonprofit leader survey participant

Is the pervasive presence and dominance of work in our lives an informed and consensual decision? The growing literature and public discourse on burnout would indicate the answer is a resounding *no*.

Unless we create new workplace cultures and structures that recognize the full humanity of all workers, any effort to decenter white supremacy and decolonize our practices will continue to be met with forceful backlash, which too often leads to racial burnout. Mistinguette Smith defines racial burnout in this way:

A person is vulnerable to racial burnout when they are constantly aware of both the micro and the meta—conscious of racism in interpersonal interactions and aware of the overwhelming structural reinforcements for white supremacy. This intense awareness creates emotional exhaustion and isolation from others who don't "get" it.[8]

One part of how we can deal with racial burnout, Smith argues, is through creating communities of support. I have found this true in my life and for many other leaders of color I have spoken to. Informal and formal affinity groups and peer women leaders of color provide a sense of mental and emotional well-being, safety, and respite when the bone-deep exhaustion of racial burnout takes hold. For me, this has happened through friendships that have lasted decades and through impromptu huddles at meetings with other women of color, where we can safely debrief and, sadly, often share how white-dominant culture and supremacy have aggressed against us.

A different but complementary perspective is shared by Rachel Hislop in "'It's Not Just Burnout:' How Grind Culture Fails Women," where she shares her personal story of leaving a CEO job and asserts, "Burnout is not only about work; it's about the flaws in our approach to work and the low value our full lives hold in the scheme of capitalism."[9] The U.S. Bureau of Labor Statistics finds that between 2020 and 2022, while the loss in male workers fully rebounded, the country lost one million women from the labor market. It is notable that working mothers, Black women, and women in senior leadership positions are overrepresented among those who left the workplace.[10]

Finally, Dany Sigwalt asserts that although burnout results from systemic issues long in the making, we have "pushed [it] behind closed doors and turned [it] into a private problem for individuals to solve using their resources."[11] This is a critical observation: Burnout is something that is done to us by the systems and structures we have intentionally and repeatedly chosen in our society. No amount of action at the individual or "self" level can counter or resist the cumulative impact of systemic and structural levels of harm and anti-wellness policies and practices that surround us. Just like with imposter syndrome, burnout is not a personal-level failing or weakness or shortcoming; it is a structural violence done to us at a population level that we are told is an individual-level responsibility.

Emphasizing the importance of workplace culture and structure, research presented in "Authenticity at Work: A Matter of Fit?" indicates that workers who feel they can be their full selves at work experience greater motivation and engagement at work and lower levels of burnout.[12] The need for psychological safety at work is foundational.

While this book speaks about women of color as a broad group, in exploring ways to dismantle current systems and create new ones, we must account for the fact that, as Cristina Alcalde and Mangala Subramaniam state, "position and location in terms of gender identity, class, racial and ethnic background, migration status, and different abilities are the basis of the experiences of women of color across layers of leadership. These intersecting identities shape career trajectories, the leadership positions women of color are expected or allowed to inhabit, and the roles they fulfill, which are frequently stereotyped in gendered and racialized ways."[13]

To support culture change and nurture the leaders who are facilitating it, we must collectively create spaces that acknowledge the positionality of women of color leaders in society and workplaces—including the specific contexts within which Black, Brown, Indigenous, trans, queer, immigrant, and refugee, and women with disabilities must each operate. Wilnelia Rivera's words say it well:

> Too often, when women of color are the leaders, we expect them to do everything. We want them to manage the emotional labor. We want them to create the systems. We want them to execute the work . . . We need to deconstruct what we're asking of leaders. We need to create a culture where we're asking other people to step up. We can't build systems that ask women of color to do more with less. That's actually what we do. Every single time! We've always created change with less. Imagine what we could do if we were supported.[14]

My hope is for this book to contribute to a sense of community, of being seen and heard, and to create spaces safe from racial gaslighting. As Danielle, a Black nonprofit leader, said, "...how much we need each other and how much this is like food for the soul. It is. And it never ceases to amaze me that . . . when we get together in generosity of spirit and rooted in our values and our core purpose, it ends up being so generative and positive. I have yet to walk away from a leadership gathering, a convening, where there is a critical mass of women of color and not felt like I was better because of it." When describing the type of workplace that would be nurturing to them and their leadership style, many of the women I spoke to mentioned working with other women of color as an essential dimension.

"I love where I work because I know I am seen and valued. I know that my input matters when I give input during a project or meeting. I know that my contributions matter. I know I don't have to work twice as hard every day to be valued like in other organizations. I don't have to expend energy on ensuring I and my abilities don't threaten my manager. I also don't have to expend energy on making others comfortable."

—LATINE, Asian American survey participant

SECTION 5

Leading Outside the Lines

*"My leadership is tied to the experiences and
the needs of those at the margins."*

—Black educational leader survey participant

W e have been working in the U.S. under very limited models for what counts as work, progress, success, leadership, and community. *There are other ways.*

Leadership is significantly shaped by life experiences, worldviews, cultural norms, organizational structure and culture, and the ability to adapt. For me, how I lead is deeply informed by the experience of being an immigrant and the adaptability and openness that demands; it is shaped by the collectivist cultural norms of my culture of origin and by the violence, inequality, and instability I experienced around me growing up in Peru. It is shaped by how I have been treated by multiple institutions that asserted my otherness and outsiderness through various forms of aggression. I experience leadership as embodied movement, and my movement continues to evolve as I unlearn lies and self-destructive biases and learn about others' realities and histories, providing context and texture to my history.

How and why I lead is about holding space for other people's growth and voices, and in that way, my leadership has been nurtured by how I mother, rejecting the artificial distinction between personal and work-life values. In my experience, mothering demands humility, curiosity, creativity, and, above all, capacity for love (including self-love). My greatest role as a mother is to love vulnerably while holding space to co-create conditions that support my children in becoming kind, fair, self-aware, and adaptable humans. Mothering, like leadership, is dynamic; it's relational and about movement, aligning various concurrent rhythms while learning and changing in ever-evolving ways. In many ways, I've found mothering and leadership to be about self-awareness and self-leadership, an existential dance between clear-eyed abjuration of the illusion of control and the disciplined practice of active empathy.[1] It is a dance, and in this dance, you don't dance alone. As a dear friend I interviewed for this book said, "You can't lead by yourself . . ."

I move to the rhythm of emergence,
    with the rise
        and the fall,
    the calm that conceals tumult,
        the shape-shifting of water,
            This is how I meet the world.

Our current leadership concepts are narrow, outdated, and built over centuries from a foundation of conquest-obsessed, extravagantly violent Christian Eurocentric narratives. Our path to a new world requires curious, humble, pragmatic, adaptive, and creative leaders who prioritize making space for others, especially those whose voices have not been listened to (or, more likely, have been silenced). The women I spoke to all had clear ideas, lessons, and models that guide their leadership at workplaces. I want to share their visions and practice of leadership with you.

Leadership Reimagined

*"It's about having a vision; it's about mobilizing and motivating
people behind a movement or cause and . . . speaking up on
behalf of those who may not have a voice."*

—SHANTI, Asian American nonprofit leader

"A leader is someone who opens new paths for others," one survey participant offered. Another described leadership as *"the ability to help others
ignite their fire."* Yet another wrote: *"I believe most leadership and leadership programs are focused on benefits to the individual. My form of leadership is focused on relationships and the advancement of the collective."*

Similarly, Krista, a Black nonprofit leader, shared, *"I think that for me,
the most important part of leadership is building people up or supporting
people to be their best selves, and that typically means being behind the scenes
and being like the unseen part, right?"*

Emilia, a Latine educational leader, synthesized what many other
women had said in describing a leader as *"someone who can envision progress not only individually, but for others on their team, and more broadly
within the structure of the workplace; someone who can support others and
push others toward a joint vision, both in developing that vision and imple-
menting it; and who can stand up to those with more power and **for and with**
those with less power."*

Idalia Fernandez and Lori Bartczak echo the ideas shared by interview
participants in their piece "Leadership Development Programs Need an
Upgrade: Five Ways to Advance Racial Equity": "Leadership is not static,
and it doesn't sit with one person. Instead, leadership is about building
collective power to influence and change organizations and systems to
operate in just and liberating ways that enable all individuals to thrive."[2]

Collectivity and community are key elements of how the women I
interviewed and surveyed understood and practiced leadership:

"A leader is somebody that doesn't see themselves as doing all the work themselves but, working in collaboration, in a team, in a community . . . everyone-at-the-table kind of leadership."

—ALEJANDRA, Latine philanthropic leader

Our emerging future does not need more hero-leaders. And let's not forget, as Deborah Bae and Kiernan Doherty tell us in "The Need for More Inclusive Leadership Narratives": "The deeply entrenched notion of a leader as an individual hero is not accidental. Many individuals and organizations with positional power want to maintain the status quo—rooted in racism, colonialism, sexism, and other 'isms'—of who has power and who has a voice."[3] Said another way by an interview participant,

"For me, embodying my power, the only power that perhaps I have, is the power to evolve myself, to humble myself, of intentionally not holding the power that is given to me but that I share it and transform it."

—ALICIA, Latine nonprofit leader

As Hanieh Khosroshahi writes, "From leadership qualities to performance reviews, our metrics for evaluating competence, skill level, and potential are centered on whiteness and are heavily skewed to favor masculinity."[4] Ly-Xiong emphasizes that leading for social change is necessarily collective and that putting the responsibility of change on an individual sets the person and the organization for failure. Ly-Xiong offers an alternative, stating, "For a social sector organization or any other system to do this, it must ask: Are we prepared to make room for people to practice leadership in ways that differ from conventional management styles? Are we prepared to adapt to and embody transformative change so that individual leaders can succeed, and so the whole organization can become more just, innovative, and open?"[5] Many of the women I interviewed reflected this sentiment, including Alicia, a Latine nonprofit leader: *"For me, it will be how do we dismantle this idea of someone making all the decisions and someone having the last word and someone saying this is the way that we should do things rather than saying okay, we are a team; we hold each other in solidarity; we honor each other's talents; and, at the same time, we hold each other accountable."*

Leadership, like power, must be dynamic and emergent for organizations, systems, and structures to be changed. Change relies on human connections being created, sustained, and altered, so leading for change must also be supported by nurturing internal and external connections. Leading in this way is not easy. I believe that to create a new reality for ourselves, we must change how we come together.

"Being willing to step into what is uncomfortable over and over again . . . and to take up space."

—KIARA, Black philanthropic leader

In examining how we organize ourselves, we must interrogate the assumptions and expectations in the concept and practice of leadership. We must ask ourselves and our institutions *Why?* and *Why not?* to build a practice of challenging invisible and calcified cultural tenets.

"A leader will have to do and say things people don't like all the time. That means everyone's not gonna like you . . ."

—ANGELA, Black nonprofit leader

For me and the women of color I have spoken with, leadership is about integrating experiences, identities, values, and various forms of sensing available to us. Part of our shared experience is that we are not the picture of how leadership is imagined in the U.S. *"So being a leader and being a woman of color is contradictory for many people,"* stated Lucia, a Latine educational leader.

Many of the women I spoke to and surveyed stated that leadership is not just for those in executive positions or positions traditionally viewed as leaders. A few women specified that they don't equate specific roles or management functions with leadership.

"How are you defining a woman who is a leader? By title? Position? What about the informal leadership roles that WOC have in organizations?"

—LATINE, Asian-American survey participant

As Don Waisanen states in *Leadership Standpoints*, "As many organizational structures become flatter and more team-based, the demands for distributing leadership among staff have increased. Smaller nonprofits, where employees perform many roles, only heighten this need."[6] Leadership is as dynamic and evolving as it is contextual and positional. Ly-Xiong puts it beautifully: "If, instead, we see leadership as a matter of finding and following new paths in collaboration with others, then it is more about understanding interactions among people and their environments and navigating a variety of unpredictable situations along the way. Creating systems change, therefore, lies not in looking to a single person but in engaging people to connect and lead together through the unknown."[7] *Yes, so much, yes.*

"I see many steps ahead, because I have to."

—Multiracial survey participant

There is no shortage of leadership models, theories, and frameworks—and none of them alone should be used prescriptively, or without the understanding that they were most likely not developed with the experiences, conditions, or visions of women of color in mind. We need more writing, research, and discussion about women of color's leadership. In the meantime, a 2022 article by Darren Isom, Cora Daniels, and Britt Savage offers some concrete lessons from leaders of color, making a meaningful contribution to our understanding of workplace leadership. "What Everyone Can Learn from Leaders of Color" states,

> The ways people of color have experienced the world up to this point can affect how they lead. This goes beyond experiences of oppression or historic marginalization to include the connection, meaning, and joy these

leaders can draw on from their respective cultures and communities. As a result, there are assets and skills many leaders of color develop and excel at because of the experiences and perspective their identity brings.[8]

Yes, let's not forget about the joy and strength.

The way that women of color experience the world equips them with specific skills and assets, described in the article as more community-centered motivations, the ability to work across identities and networks, and being particularly adept at change management—which involves possessing "self-awareness," seeing the world with "double consciousness" and from the perspective of "intersectional identities," being "comfortable [with] being uncomfortable," having "a high degree of empathy," "observation and active listening," "collaborative leadership," "asset-based approach[es]," and "radical imagination."[9]

Leadership can be liberating when it grows from a deep commitment to learning how to use power without becoming a power over, domination, or oppression in its relationships. The women I spoke to called out power over as something they are specifically and intentionally working to undo. Power over is not the only way to manifest agency and vision; power over constricts breath and creativity and inevitably causes harm and dehumanizes all parties, depriving us of possibility. Leadership that nurtures co-creation requires that we learn to sit with discomfort, differentiate safety from comfort, and recognize the messiness of change not as a failure but as fertile opportunities for growth.

CHAPTER 19

Dreaming of a New Way

Leading with the four Cs

"We can do so much more and be so much better . . . There's another world for us, one in which we don't deal with the competition, a workplace that fosters our growth."

—KRISTA, Black nonprofit leader

As with leadership, there are multiple models and frameworks for organizing ourselves for work. A full exploration of these models is beyond the scope of this book, but I will name and share briefly some of the ideas and concepts that influence my thinking and that of the women I interviewed.

First, the way forward must grow from our integral commitment to shared values. When we see the dissonance between what is possible and what we are doing, it is unethical to continue doing things as they have always been done. It is in *how* we engage with each other, *how* we manifest our values, *how* we arrange ourselves, and *how* we translate our visions for the future into current-day practices so that deep social change can take root. I have personally found these four traits, the *four Cs*, essential to culture change work at organizations:

curiosity

creativity

courage

care

Leadership can and should help create the conditions for these four Cs to be cultural expectations at work. Creating the conditions for the four Cs to take root requires creating structures and infrastructures to make curiosity, creativity, courage, and care possible, incentivizing them, making them second nature, and making them part of the culture. The four Cs are, at once, necessary for and supported by anti-supremacist culture and practices.

People who have had to exist in the world in a way that requires them to

be **curious** to understand a dominant culture that doesn't represent them or their experiences

use **creativity** to bridge and translate across cultures, experiences, and perspectives

have **courage** to keep showing up and speaking up in contexts that make them invisible (or hyper-visible), silenced or unsupported, and all too often, contexts that make them unsafe, and

care for themselves and their community, as societal structures tend to abuse and neglect all perceived as *the other*,

may more readily tap into the discipline of the four Cs. Although these competencies may be more readily available to women of color, everyone benefits from working in cultures that nurture and support the four Cs— and everyone can develop a practice of leading with the four Cs.

Organizations often confuse existential moments of paradox, which invite creativity, integration, and innovation, with binary dilemmas, which generally lead to either/or and zero-sum approaches. Because women of color leaders live in a world of paradox, we excel in spaces created to exclude us and our gifts, and we have extensive practice in adaptability, emergence, seeing beyond the binary, and engaging with tension and the spaces in between in ways that can open new paths for institutions and organizations. We are creative, courageous, and adaptive by necessity.

Are these values you experience in your workplace? Can you think of ways to bring each of these four values into practice in your workplace? What structures, policies, practices, and conversations would be needed to bring the four Cs to your workplace and to nurture these competencies in your team?

Power

> *"Power is not only the collective capacity to influence resources and policy. Power is also an 'inside job' from our collective convictions that we discover when we imagine together and heal our insecurities and fears."*

—SHAWN A. GINWRIGHT, *The Four Pivots*

Power is at the core of all my conversations with the women I interviewed, and in any conversation about change, justice, and freedom. Liberated leadership requires awareness of power and how it is operating at any time and space. As quoted in Waisanen's *Leadership Standpoints*, "Many of the gravest problems in our world—from climate change to inequality to child abuse—are rooted in the misuse of power."[1] Power is not, in and of itself, problematic; how we have chosen to distribute and use it is. As Cyndi Suarez states in *The Power Manual*, "Power is, first of all, relational . . . Power is not about the rule of law, institutions, society, or the state. These are simply the dead forms, or artifacts, that result from past power-laden interactions or confrontations."[2]

Power can come from a place of love or a place of fear. One can tap into *power within* and *power with*, as part of what JASS calls transformational power.[3] This is where rooting in our values and building our structures and processes in alignment with our values and our commitment to love are essential. I recommend exploring the concept of vulnerable power, the understanding that "only by exercising power in such a way as to make ourselves vulnerable to transformation can we hope to encourage voluntary transformation in others rather than mere conformity, compliance, or resistance."[4] With this conception of power, liberated workplace cultures will allow us to nurture leaders who are supported in their full-ness of "vulnerability and . . . courage . . . both fierce and kind."[5] In liber-ated spaces, the practice of freedom is possible and necessarily "includes both the refusal to be dominated and the refusal to dominate."[6]

The misuse of power (power over) is the root of many of our world's problems. But the vision of a way forward is grounded in love and solidar-ity, which rely upon power with and power within. It might sound trite to some, but at its essence, human existence is about love in all its forms and permutations. In this section, I explore and share some ways in which people, organizations, and systems have worked to reinvent themselves in service of justice and liberation. These are models for how we can mani-fest love in the public spheres.

The women I interviewed all talked about power in different ways, but all of them distinguished between traditional power (power over) and *power with*. They drew a connection between embodying their power and power as being in service to their communities and a shared purpose. They spoke of how they understand power and how they embodied power:

"Embodying power means a challenge to traditional power; it means being able to think of how you can use your talents and your skills, to be able to challenge the status quo and to move things in a different direc-tion, in ways that are not necessarily acknowledged."

"As women of color, the relationship that we have with power in the world is complicated, it's different . . . For me, embodying power is understand-ing what you bring to the table and owning that . . . and not trying to do all the things because we can't do all the things. Part of embodying your power is knowing your weaknesses and then building your team, your circle, your tribe, or whatever, around that knowledge."

"My lived experience gives me power."

"To embody power is to know yourself so well that you're not intimidated by another person's way of doing things."

"I have realized that part of who I am, because of my personal survival story . . . my power, is to speak the truth, the truth of my experience, the truth of my survival."

The Importance of Engaging with Structures

Structure is both technical and adaptive; it is the crux where culture translates into strategy and vice versa, where it gets messy and uncomfortable. Structure is beyond the realm of the narrowly professional, as it engages core self, beliefs, long-held practices and assumptions, and positionality. One challenge I've heard many times is around the oversimplification of equity and structures: leaders shared that as they work toward making their workplace more equitable and they change their organizational structure, staff often equate equity in structure to having a "flat" structure.

In other words, people can see any acknowledgment of differences among team members as necessarily inequitable. I think we are experiencing the same confusion we experience with power: power in and of itself, just like difference, is not inequitable. How these concepts are often used and applied is inequitable. I also find it surprising that equity in structure is conceived by many as everyone being treated the same, given that one of the critical dimensions of equity is that it is *not* the same as equality. *Equity recognizes and engages with difference.* Pretending everyone is the same is not only unrealistic in most organizations but also harmful because it does not reflect reality. We can have organizations that acknowledge differences and treat everyone with respect and dignity. I view organizational structure as multidimensional, not flat, more of a constellation than a one-dimensional pyramid or flat line.

"My desire to have shared power, decision-making, and building consensus is unusual."

—Asian American survey participant

A fabulous piece about organizational structure by Jeanne Bell, "Why Staff Structure Matters (A Lot)," addresses questions and criticisms about putting so much energy into changing structures while asserting the collective nature of culture-making and the essential role structure plays:

> Why are we adapting our structures so often? Isn't that inefficient? There are at least two extraordinarily valid reasons:
>
> 1. Traditional, corporate structures rarely produce the equity, transparency, accelerated leadership development, and meaningful innovation that justice-committed staff and leadership crave. We are compelled to experiment with variations or even stark alternatives to those traditional structures to produce more of what we value for and from our staff.
>
> 2. In justice-committed organizations, strategies are ambitious, complex, and ever-evolving. As our understanding of the work in front of us changes, we are compelled to reconfigure ourselves to get the needed perspectives around the table, to ask the emergent questions, and to adapt our work accordingly.[7]

Structures, notably, include processes, such as decision-making. Structures responsive to changing conditions and realities recognize that power must be dynamic to avoid getting stuck and impeding growth and change. Creativity is essential in experimenting with structures and dynamic power to reflect our values.

Notwithstanding, as we dream, experiment, and learn together, we must not confuse the appearance of new ways of working with true transformation. Organizations may adopt tools and structures that signal justice and equity while holding on to cultural norms and practices that keep white patriarchy alive and well. In her essay for Community-Centric Fundraising "What Working at a Flat Organization Has Taught Me about White Supremacy," Yolanda Contreras offers her experience in an organization that adopted a so-called flat structure. Although the organization shifted to what it conceived as a nonhierarchical structure, white supremacy was still very much present in how people were treated and in the power dynamics beyond the organizational chart. Contreras explains, "In the absence of bosses, time and again, it's the white people that try to step up and act like they're the ones in charge. BIPOC have always been told that we are not the ones to lead, yet white people don't seem to have any reservations about assuming leadership roles. They seem unable to let go of traditional harmful practices because they want and need these power structures in place—because it directly benefits them."[8] Her story offers an important warning: structural change without attendant culture change cannot do away with deeply held cultural norms, such as supremacist tendencies.

Maurice Mitchell speaks to the threat of superficial organizational shifts in the excellent article "Building Resilient Organizations":

> It's easier to use language and cultural references that signify an ideological inclination than to study and practice a particular framework. However, such loose ideological signaling can lead to incoherence. This practice can devolve legitimate frameworks, concepts, and language into tools for individuals to virtue signal or provide weight to an argument that does not stand on its premises. It should be noted that it is popular to borrow catchphrases and quotes from Black feminists, theorists, thinkers, and collectives. This is especially pernicious when the arguments those thinkers developed are hijacked and flattened by those seeking personal benefit or legitimacy.[9]

CHAPTER 20

Dimensions of Care, Rest, and Healing

"Just as nonprofits prioritize care for the people they serve, they must reorient their management practices to integrate caring into their organizations."

—ELIZABETH CASTILLO, "Walking the Talk: Reclaiming Dignity through Humanistic Management"

Self-care and collective care are necessary for our work toward collective healing and liberation. To varying degrees and consistency, we have all experienced individual and collective harm and carry that trauma down generations. So we must heal both individually and collectively, and to do so, we have to push beyond Calvinist and puritanical resistance to healing, joy, and rest.

Self-care is essential and pragmatic for women of color leaders: as Brené Brown's research has shown, "who we are is how we lead." So working on healing ourselves is vital to us as people, as leaders, and to the organizations, movements, and communities we serve and are members of. In her piece "Rest Is Restorative, Healing," Bethany Johnson-Javois speaks to the importance of rest, especially as, for too many, "work is labor that takes a toll on the body, mind, and spirit." She affirms, "Rest is restorative and healing; it is resistance to the capitalistic culture of profit over people."[1]

I am on a (likely long and nonlinear) journey of renegotiating my relationship with rest and caring for myself, my body, and beyond. The more I invest in caring for myself in how I care for others, the more I believe that rest is essential to our long-term liberation and a key aspect of good leadership. I recently finished Tricia Hersey's *Rest Is Resistance: A Manifesto*, and felt every word she spoke rings true while also being radical for our mainstream workplace culture. Through the Nap Ministry, Hersey is gifting us with the message, the truth, that "our worth is not connected to how much we produce" and that "another way is possible."[2]

And while self-care, self-love, and self-compassion are necessary for healing and growth, they can never be the sole solution to our systemic problems. Systemic and societal-level harms require systemic and societal-level healing. This is a situation for *both/and*, not either/or. The personal and cultural levels of work are connected and intertwined, as Yonason Goldson reminds us in their piece "This Is the Secret to Healing a Toxic Culture": "It's easy for individuals to convince themselves that their little actions have no appreciable impact on work environments"[3] and, therefore, convince ourselves that there is nothing we can do or are already doing to change or maintain workplace culture. The article goes on to list a variety of areas in which organizations that rank high on a sense of trust excel, linking trust and safety explicitly: workers report having more energy at work, feeling more aligned with workplace purpose, feeling closer to coworkers, more engagement and productivity, being more likely to stay at the job, more empathy for coworkers, and, importantly, being significantly less likely to experience burnout.

Trust

"I lead with trust."

—Asian American survey participant

Trust is a practice that requires transparency, accountability, empathy, and power-aware interactions. Trust is not the same as niceness or having positive intentions toward your peers and communities; trust is a practice that requires intentional awareness and engaging with growth opportunities.[4] Carolyn O'Hara sums up "Proven Ways to Earn Your Employees' Trust": "Create a personal connection . . . be transparent and truthful . . . encourage rather than command . . . take blame, give credit . . . don't play favorites . . . show competence."[5] She makes it clear that these must be practices at the interpersonal level and evident in policies at the organizational level. The Trust-Based Philanthropy Project offers many resources to encourage and support philanthropy in shifting its practices, cultures, structures, and leadership approaches toward trust and equity, and, in that way, change both the philanthropic and nonprofit sectors.

> *"Power is in relationships; power is earned from trust,*
> *not linked with title or hierarchy"*
>
> —Survey participant

As we co-create new models for working together and new ways of organizing ourselves, let us remember the simple and beautiful truth that "Joy is the most vulnerable and courageous emotion."[6] Meanwhile, I will continue processing Hersey's *Rest Is Resistance*, challenging internal beliefs and (de)programming mental settings about productivity, rest, laziness, and deservingness, and relearning to trust myself.

Community and Culture

> *"We're part of a collective, and we've come from cultures that are collective,*
> *community-based cultures. So, it's not like I just do this thing for me . . . it's*
> *about my survival, my community's survival, my ancestors' survival."*
>
> —DANIELLE, Black nonprofit leader

As we intentionally and consciously create a culture beyond white supremacy, we can liberate our ideas beyond binary thinking and siloed efforts and give way to emergence and, with it, the possibility of integration. A common theme in the conversations I had with women of color was the collective nature of the work and the centrality of community. Reviewing the themes of the interviews reminded me of something I'd read about Maslow's hierarchy of needs and how the Siksika culture and way of life influenced him. Contrary to what Maslow had hypothesized, "he did not see the quest for [interpersonal] dominance in Blackfoot society. Instead, he discovered astounding levels of cooperation, minimal inequality, restorative justice, full bellies, and high levels of life satisfaction." He estimated that "80–90% of the Blackfoot tribe had a quality of self-esteem only found in 5–10% of his population."[7]

Interestingly, in Maslow's hierarchy of needs as we know it, self-actualization is the highest level we aspire to, unlike in the Blackfoot community. As Teju Ravilochan states, "Whereas mainstream American narratives focus on the individual, the Blackfoot way of life offers an alternative resulting in a community that leaves no one behind."[8] A community that leaves no one behind is the dream I work toward. The following quote from Ravilochan's article "The Blackfoot Wisdom That Inspired Maslow's Hierarchy" beautifully captures how every woman I spoke to described their understanding and practice of leadership: "As Maslow witnessed in the Blackfoot Giveaway, many First Nation cultures see the work of meeting basic needs, ensuring safety, and creating the conditions for the expression of purpose as a community responsibility, not an individual one."[9]

Leading in a way that is beyond the individual or individualistic is about working in service of shared values, of community, and a future yet unknown. It is also leading with the past in mind:

> "Power sometimes has a negative connotation, but I think that for many of us, it's not about reclaiming our power, but it's about reclaiming the power that our ancestors were denied. And so I think, for me, embodying power is speaking truth. I think it's about putting voice to truth."
>
> —SHANTI, Asian American nonprofit leader

Part of the work ahead involves reframing the why and the how of work to include collective work and care. In other words, we must understand collective healing as part of the path to changing culture. Collective healing in and of itself is a transformation from injury to wholeness. There are different ways to think about culture change and many theories and schools of thought. Before we can change culture, we must understand what culture entails:

- Values, or what we care about
- Norms, such as the explicit structures, processes, and (little p and big P) policies that reinforce values
- Behaviors, or the daily actions that manifest our values

Working to change workplace culture engages with all three dimensions—values, norms, and behaviors—offering multiple dimensions and pathways to work on collective healing.

Another way to think about healing in workplaces is as healing justice. Loretta Pyles, in *Healing Justice: Holistic Self-Care for Change Makers*, describes healing justice as "a framework that identifies how we can holistically respond to and intervene on generational trauma and violence and bring collective practices that can impact and transform the consequences of oppression on our bodies, hearts, and minds."[10]

Organizations must work at the culture level to change themselves and address root assumptions about power, race, and gender. Changes at the culture level will one day mean that going to work will be a safer place for *everyone*. While organizations often get stuck in fear of change and frame DEI work as beneficial solely or primarily to BIPOC workers, the reality is that making our workplaces more humane benefits everyone. Like the curb-cut effect—where the addition of curb cuts to sidewalks, brought about as a result of tireless work by disability advocates, has benefited countless others in easier and safer mobility—"laws and programs designed to benefit vulnerable groups, such as the disabled or people of color, often end up benefiting all of society."[11]

Angela Glover Blackwell sums it up perfectly in her 2017 piece "The Curb-Cut Effect":

> There's an ingrained societal suspicion that intentionally supporting one group hurts another. That equity is a zero-sum game. In fact, when the nation targets support where it is needed most—when we create the circumstances that allow those who have been left behind to participate and contribute fully—everyone wins. The corollary is also true: When we ignore the challenges faced by the most vulnerable among us, those challenges, magnified many times over, become a drag on economic growth, prosperity, and national well-being.[12]

Taking Care of Self to Care for Community

But we don't, and shouldn't, just exist for work. Transformative change will necessitate cultural metamorphosis across all dimensions of our worlds. While this book is focused on the changes that organizations and their cultures must undertake, it is impossible to talk about changing organizations and their cultures without talking about changing ourselves and healing our wounds. For a deep dive into healing from racial trauma in the workplace, I recommend Minda Harts's book *Right Within*.

Each of us is connected to, not separate or impervious to, what happens all around us: at home, at work, in our communities, in our country, around the world, and to our planet. The inherent interconnectedness among us all and all the levels at which we exist gives us a window to empathy, solidarity, and collective liberation. This interconnectedness can also drain us from accumulated personal and vicarious harm, neglected compassion and unreciprocated empathy, and shutting out adjurations for wholeness. I hope you'll know and remember these words of Audre Lorde: *"Caring for myself is not self-indulgence; it is self-preservation, and that is an act of political warfare."*[13]

Feeling invisible and unheard was pervasive among the women I spoke to. When we're talking about changing systems, beliefs, and power structures that have not only existed for generations but have shackled, murdered, and dehumanized countless souls with impunity, it can and will feel overwhelming.

As Yashna Maya Padamsee says in "Communities of Care, Organizations for Liberation," *"If we let ourselves be caught up in the discussion of self-care, we are missing the whole point of healing justice work. . . . Too often self-care in our organizational cultures gets translated to our individual responsibility to leave work early, go home—alone—and go take a bath, go to the gym, eat some food and go to sleep. So we do all of that 'self-care' to return to organizational cultures where we reproduce the systems we are trying to break."*[14] And let's be clear: the ability to take time off from work, while necessary, is not liberation; it is not a stand-in for collective care or just workplace culture. As Anne Helen Petersen says, "If you have the means, you can go on temporary vacation from that brokenness—as we did. But it's still waiting to envelop you when you return."[15]

Because harm begets harm, we must create structures and organizations that do not harm their internal communities and are part of and connected to a broader system that can provide for their internal and external communities' essential needs and human rights. Mariame Kaba shares this simple but central truth: *"Understanding that harm originates from situations dominated by stress, scarcity, and oppression, one way to prevent violence is to make sure that people have support to get the things they need."*[16] Humans need to have basic needs met; humans need rest; we need safe workplaces, living places, play places, and learning places; we need to get unstuck and co-create new healing cultures where we can all thrive.

CHAPTER 21

Beyond Us and Now

I do not believe I will see the changes I dream of in my lifetime, but that is not discouraging. It is calming. I can only contribute my small piece, and together with others across time and space, we will transform our shared reality. The realization that I am but a small, seemingly insignificant force gives me purpose and allows me to give myself and others some grace. No person needs to carry it all, and no one person can. Tina Turner was right: "We don't need another hero." We need each other, whether we like it or not. Change is collective work, healing is collective work, and it often does not go as planned, but as Dolly Parton says, "We cannot direct the wind, but we can adjust the sails."

Moving Toward the Unknown

As we make our way toward liberatory leadership, we will encounter countless barriers and resistance. Some of the challenges that we can anticipate as we move toward instituting a collectivist, solidarity-rooted approach include

- hyper-individualism distracting from collective work at the communal level
- competition undermining the collaboration required for liberatory social structures and obscuring the interdependence of all living things
- resistance to ceding or sharing power
- narrow conceptions of excellence

- turfism or imperialism of work territory
- a sense of security drawn from individual exceptionalism
- success viewed and defined through an individual lens
- traditional and paternalistic governance models
- narrow and shallow conceptions of how we understand and assess impact
- notions of productivity derived from unfettered capitalism
- wealth as wisdom, and wealth as power
- presumed deference to those with positional power
- power viewed as individually held rather than collective, shared, or distributed
- power seen as static, stable, and inherited, rather than dynamic and fluid

In our current reality, workplaces are not spaces of consensual participation. In a country where health care and basic needs are tied to work, there is no true choice or freedom in work. Particularly for populations who continue to experience exploitation, oppression, and violence, workplaces extend lack of freedom by tying essential needs to hierarchical institutions in a white-supremacist and patriarchal model. While many changes can be made to workplaces and institutions to decrease the harm inherent in their structures and processes (cultures), true movement away from extractive and exploitative workplaces will require policy changes that allow all people to provide for their basic needs without dependence on employers.

Exploring the policy changes needed for liberated workplaces is beyond the scope of this book. Still, I will name that without equitable and universal access to comprehensive health care, housing, education, child care, transportation, and paid time off from work, as well as policy protections for equal pay, safe and fair working conditions, and protections from discrimination, changes within workplaces will be limited and disjointed from broader society. Nonetheless, sustainable and transformative social change requires movement from multiple points in time and space, and changing workplace cultures is an essential dimension of the necessary orchestrated change.

Despite all the challenges and criticisms of workplaces in this book, "we need institutions for a powerful and durable movement. Organizations and institutions are political vehicles. They are also spaces where individuals develop skills, connections, and ideological alignment. Institutions transmit knowledge, hold strategy, and cultivate power," as Maurice Mitchell says in "Building Resilient Organizations."[1]

We are moving toward the unknown and imagining new ways of constructing workplaces. There are endless models, experiments, and dreams of new ways of organizing ourselves around labor, but the paths to a new future will be emergent, at times parallel and intersecting, too, and we must adapt and change as our contexts and understanding evolve. I will share some ideas that most align with what I and the women I spoke to are working to create. These concepts and models can serve as explorations, inspiration, and guides.

An Open Invitation: Let's Dream

"Liberation is 1,000 little experiments, not models."

—TRISH TCHUME, "Experiments in Liberatory Leadership"

I have not provided a ready-to-consume model for a new type of organization or workplace culture. I offer no new catchphrases to replace previous catchphrases. I recognize that we've all been conditioned to want the answer, the solution, the punch line. And I believe that is part of the recurring problem with our approach to leadership and organizations. *Structures and cultures are alive*; they are dynamic and emergent, which takes ongoing work and awareness. We must approach the work of culture change as *a relationship with change.* The concepts and frameworks I share here can inform, feed, and inspire your imagination on how workplaces can construct themselves to birth values-based cultures. Co-creating new workplace cultures will happen organically, intentionally, and collectively with those you work with. Your relationship with change will evolve, as all relationships do.

What follows is not an exhaustive list but some resources that intrigued me and might whet your imagination. Let these concepts spark your curiosity.

Buen vivir. Buen vivir is a social philosophy that "describes a way of doing things that is community-centric, ecologically-balanced and culturally-sensitive" and has roots in the Indigenous Andean world-view of sumak kawsay.[2] This worldview has many similarities to decolonization: questioning traditional approaches to development, centering on the interconnectedness of all things, and challenging capitalism. I invite you to read about buen vivir and see how it relates to your values.

Community. Ponder what community means to you, where you learned about community, and how many communities you belong to, simultaneously or sequentially. Read about different cultural understandings of community, and consider how they inform and shape policies, norms, and institutions. Explore collectivist perspectives and practices of community. Community is at the core of everything living things do.

Solidarity. In the U.S., the ethical principle of solidarity is less talked about than in many other parts of the world, to our detriment. Solidarity is connected to the concept of community and collectivism. You can get a good dive into the ethical principle of solidarity in Borna Jalsenjak's article "Principle of Solidarity," where solidarity is defined as "a socio-ethical and political concept which states that it is fair and just that benefits and obligations are justly shared between members of the society."[3]

Various concepts of power. In my research, interviews, and conversations for and about this book, different concepts of power—particularly power over, power with, and power within—came up from multiple sources. I reference Cyndi Suarez's *The Power Manual* quite a bit. There is much to read about power; keep an open yet critical mind.

Dynamic power. I have long believed that how we think about power leads to developing and practicing organizational structures and leadership approaches that ignore the fact that nothing is static, certainly not power. Where and how power is held should be informed by the specific circumstance where it will be applied. I found Daniela Blei's piece "Diversity, Hierarchy, and Teamwork" engaging with this concept of dynamic power in a way that might be helpful to your thinking about organizations and power.[4]

Targeted universalism. Targeted universalism is a framework developed by john a. powell and the Othering & Belonging Institute at UC Berkeley.[5] I have found targeted universalism to be helpful in bringing equity into policy development and implementation, because it accounts for context relative to specific groups and populations, like driving toward a shared collective goal. The Othering & Belonging Institute describes targeted universalism as a process of setting "universal goals pursued by targeted processes to achieve those goals. Within a targeted universalism framework, universal goals are established for all groups concerned. The strategies developed to achieve those goals are targeted based on how different groups are situated within structures, cultures, and across geographies to obtain the universal goal. Targeted universalism is goal-oriented, and the processes are directed in service of the explicit, universal goal."

Ideas Arrangements Effects. This book, by Design Studio for Social Intervention, was like a nutritious and delicious smoothie for my brain—the part of my brain that loves thinking about structures, cultures, and change.[6] For a sample, take a look at the article they wrote for *Nonprofit Quarterly.*[7]

Holacracy, sociocracy, and teal organizations. Many structure models explore different forms of governance, ways of organizing ourselves, and making decisions. I have particularly enjoyed reading about these three approaches: the concept of teal organizations, developed by Laloux and based on global research on various sizes and types of organizations;[8] and the concepts of sociocracy and holacracy, which you can read about through the websites Sociocracy For All[9] and Holacracy.[10]

Shared sisterhood. Another concept that makes me smile is shared sisterhood.[11] Tina Opie and Beth Livingston developed this model to explore new organizational cultures where intersectionality is embraced through collective action to move toward equity at work. You can learn about this approach in the namesake book, which explores "how to take collective action for gender and racial equity at work."

Sensemaking organizations. Cyndi Suarez writes about the sensemaking organization, which she describes as an entity that gathers diverse groups of people guided by shared social goals to address complex social problems. "Civil sector organizations—association groups, social movements, and nonprofit organizations—especially those working for social justice, are by nature sensemaking organizations.... Not only are they sensemaking organizations, but civil sector organizations serve a sensemaking role in society. The purpose of the sector is to pay attention to the complexity of the social body and lead social change that keeps the polity relevant."[12]

There's much to explore in the journal *Nonprofit Quarterly* (*NPQ*) about alternative organizational structures, cultures, and leadership approaches, including the following concepts:

Humanistic management. Elizabeth Castillo writes about humanistic management as an approach that is "rooted in principles of dignity, care, mutual respect, and partnership rather than control and domination (Pirson, 2017) . . . humanistic management in the context of business emerged in the late nineteenth century as a counterpoint to scientific management." She goes on to say that this management approach includes practices such as: "wage equity, pay transparency, autonomy and self-managed teams, and promoting family well-being."[13] Another from *NPQ*:

Upbuilding. Tiloma Jayasinghe writes about upbuilding, which "happens when infrastructure is defined expansively, centering humans and communities, and with a strong equity, anti-oppressive lens. Upbuilding requires having the willingness and imagination to question why things are the way they are, whether they serve or oppress, and whether they can be done differently. In short, upbuilding means building something new and different as opposed to recovering and going back to 'normal.'"[14] Jayasinghe discusses a values-driven approach to creating new nonprofit structures and cultures as an alternative to the "tension between what nonprofits do and how the nonprofit itself is organized. In large part, the organizations or institutions that hold the work are built on inherently racist, oppressive structures that are not serving the people doing the work, the movement, or the communities they serve."

Dreaming. It's been said many times in this book (including the title of this section) and endless others: dreaming is essential for liberation. An exciting project moving us to reimagine philanthropy is Freedom Dreams in Philanthropy, which describes itself as "a distinct opportunity to listen to and leverage visionary leaders' voices to transform our institutions toward justice."[15]

Trust. When I did primary qualitative research for my doctoral dissertation, one of the themes identified as necessary for providing access to family planning information and services for foreign-born Latina immigrants was confianza. Confianza is commonly translated as trust. Trust has been a theme in every meaningful effort in my life, personal and professional, and I consider trust a practice that requires internal discipline, courage, and mutual accountability. I have been involved with the Trust-Based Philanthropy Project since 2021 and consider it a refuge from traditional philanthropy's paternalism and white saviorism. I believe a trust-based framework rooted in anti-racism can allow philanthropy, nonprofits, and even government to engage with each other in the service of communities.

Models from My Experience

Throughout my career, I have experimented with various structures in the places where I have worked. From my experience, two of the more interesting experiments include a grassroots reproductive justice entity and emergent staff structure at a foundation.

> **Kentucky Health Justice Network.** After our group developed bylaws and articles of incorporation and worked with a lawyer to become a 501(c)(3), we decided not to become a 501(c)(3) because we felt it was antithetical to our structure and purpose: to infuse reproductive justice knowledge and approach into other organizations, so that sustainability was about others adopting the values and knowledge inherent to reproductive justice. We didn't want our grassroots entity to become one more competitor for limited funding resources in the state. Instead, we wanted to be a partner

to other organizations. Because that was the purpose, the way we built the team to do this work was different. I first invited a close friend I had worked with before to co-lead and bring together our aligned values and very different but complementary skill sets. We then recruited people (mostly community organizers) who were already working in other social justice and social service fields and provided them with training about reproductive justice. We intentionally built a culture of support, mutuality, ongoing learning, and creativity to continue to infuse reproductive justice tenets into all community partners' organizations and institutions.

We didn't have an office; we rotated where we met, always providing child care and food for our team (and at any events we held). We collaborated with reproductive rights and health groups, identifying which approach should lead in what situation. We worked heavily on educating ourselves and others, providing resources, and connecting the dots between others' work and reproductive justice. We developed training modules for health care and social service providers; developed a program for first-generation Latin American immigrant women from a very holistic approach to reproductive and sexual health and well-being; held movie nights at peoples' homes and facilitated conversations about reproductive justice issues touched on in the films; partnered with a nonprofit media organization in a small Appalachian community where young women developed short videos and I created a facilitator's guide on a variety of reproductive justice topics that the young women creating the short videos selected; held community events that explicitly connected reproductive and environmental justice; and even worked with self-employed individuals who offered "sex toy" parties by providing them with training on reproductive justice and intimate partner violence and equipped them with a variety of brochures on various sexual and reproductive health and well-being they could share with clients safely and confidentially. We also worked on providing an informal system of support for people needing abortions, connecting them to abortion funds, transportation, interpreters, child care, and other needs.

It was an emergent organization that thrived on creativity and collaboration. It was hampered by a funder who kept trying to impose models from other countries with very different socio-political conditions, or insisted that we focus exclusively on abortion instead of taking a more holistic reproductive justice approach. Only the two directors worked full-time (although we paid ourselves for thirty and twenty hours per week to make the budget work), and everyone else worked part-time while also working at other organizations tackling domestic violence, immigrant services, economic justice, health care, education, carceral system, and social work, because of our stated purpose of integrating reproductive justice knowledge and approach into their primary work.

The community organizers lived and worked across the state, working in a loose network connected by shared values, mutual support, and commitment to responsiveness to the community. Our governance was lean, with three advisers who functioned as thought partners and connectors. Both I and the other co-director had to step away from leading the organization at around the same time, and as it transitioned to new leadership, the organization was incorporated into a 501(c)(3), and it continues to operate but with a narrower focus.

Sewall Foundation. The other example is a pod structure my team and I developed at a private, independent foundation. When I started working at the foundation, its structure was a narrow, hierarchical pyramid common in most nonprofits. Conversations with staff made it clear that the structure was not serving anyone well, and certainly not the organizational values. My goal was to distribute decision-making and leadership opportunities in a way that expanded space for creativity, limited bottlenecks and micromanaging, mitigated the difference in treatment and influence between administrative and program staff, tapped into everyone's full set of skills and passions, and exposed the organization to the leadership gifts of all staff.

We developed pods according to functional areas at the organization and experimented for a year, then identified areas for improvement. We revised the pods—adding some, removing others, and moving some to ad hoc status—and continued to work on decision-making processes. The structure remained alive, allowing for tweaks and adaptations. This more fluid and less linear structure was liberating for some staff and frustrating and confusing for others.

Nonetheless, a few years into using the pod structure, I observed that the entire team was more creative, decisions were more distributed, and most staff took more initiative and held more responsibility. Most people had expanded their role at the organization to include skills and experiences that were ignored in prior configurations. For example, in our reconfiguration, a team member who was an artist (but whose original role did not include their artistic skills) led our internal learning with data visualization and visual tools; they applied their creative thinking to learning, design, and process efforts. Another staff member, who had owned a bed and breakfast, shifted from a narrowly conceived administrative assistant role to leading the organization's human resources, facility, and vendor management.

The organization worked on aligning our values and equity principles internally and externally. We applied the triad of trust-based philanthropy, emergent learning, and equity lens frameworks to

all we did. We were co-creating something new, and we benefit-
ted from working with consultants who supported and guided us
in adopting tools and practices that clarified our roles, decision-
making, and power sharing. These structural, procedural, and
operating changes shifted the organizational culture—our team
came to recognize that "the messy middle" of deep change was
our sweet spot, as we worked to be a good partner to our community partners by supporting their work through multiple tools and
strategies. One concrete outcome was that each staff member led
one of our pods, allowing the organization to benefit from various
leadership styles and experiences.

This did not, however, make us a "flat organization." I will say that
doing work in a relational values-driven manner was more work
for all staff, and being the leader of an organization with a more
dynamic understanding of power is complex and can be challenging. Telling people what to do without concern for their views,
preferences, or opinions is easier than leading with healing, justice,
and co-creation in mind. But easier is hardly ever better, especially
when we remind ourselves that decades and centuries of cultural
imperialism have conditioned us all to consider white-supremacist,
patriarchal, capitalist, and rabidly individualistic ways the path of
least resistance.

Throughout these changes, the staff team worked to influence and support changes in the organization's governance, moving from a traditional
board to a more power-aware, policy-setting board. These changes were
not easy; they involved trying to move deeply-seated power dynamics,
and all the struggles mentioned in earlier sections of this book that show
up in resistance to change manifested over the first few years. As challenging as the changes to the staff structure were, they were easy compared to
the effort of trying to change governance practices and assumptions. Inviting people who hold power to let go of some of that power is extremely

difficult, and resistance is guaranteed, even when those involved want to change. Grounding in explicitly named and defined values is essential in the ongoing effort for sustaining cultural change.

In Closing

"Community must not mean a shedding of our differences, nor the pathetic pretense that they do not exist. It is learning how to take our differences and make them strengths. For the master's tools will never dismantle the master's house. They may allow us temporarily to beat him at his own game, but they will never allow us to bring about genuine change."

**—AUDRE LORDE, "The Master's Tools
Will Never Dismantle the Master's House"**

We must create a new world, and start by dismantling the systems that create, sustain, and profit from inequity and injustice—including outdated leadership models, organizational structures, and ideas about work. To make our differences our strengths, we must hear each other's stories and practice empathy.

Empathy lubricates the movement for social justice.

New ways of working and organizing ourselves will move us away from othering and toward each other. In my conversations with other women of color, what we long for is not just a different organization type. We want to be part of something alive, complex, and responsive. *We want to be seen. We want to exist in a place where we can be whole.* As Cyndi Suarez says, "These leaders want to explore liberatory leadership, not just institutionalize equity."[16]

Every day, we face endless invitations to choose what we practice (including inaction). Understanding that we become what we practice, we can practice solidarity, choose love as justice, and choose to be complicit in creating a world of courage, creativity, curiosity, and care even when, *especially when*, it is uncomfortable and makes us feel vulnerable. Think of it as the existential equivalent of brain science's "neurons that fire together, wire together."[17]

This is the invitation: *practice*.

Practice dreaming.

Practice identifying and staying aware of the values most vital to the world you want to live in.

Practice not turning away from discomfort.

Practice pausing instead of reacting.

Practice empathy, truly considering with your mind, heart, and body the perspective, emotions, and experience of others.

Think about the stories shared in this book; contemplate that we are real women who experienced these things; and choose to be part of the collective effort of changing our workplaces, so others don't have to keep feeling like the status quo is killing us. Practice solidarity so that, together, we can create spaces of collective care in our workplaces, in our homes, in our communities, and within ourselves.

We have what we need to shed the suffocating cloak of outdated systems and structures. We can choose creativity, courage, curiosity, and care. For ourselves, for each other, and for our planet. Together, we can create the fantastic unknown. *Let's fly.*

Survey Findings

I conducted an anonymous online survey in late 2022 into early 2023, with thirty-two women participating across the U.S. I used a passive snowballing effect to get the survey instrument into the field. This is a snapshot in time and not intended to represent the views and experiences of all women of color in the U.S. Below are the aggregated results.

What does the word "leader" mean to you?

- Change, collaboration, advocacy
- Care, seen, inspire
- Collaborator, creative, decision-maker
- Mentor
- Facilitating, role modeling, decision-making (hard to just pick 3!)
- Kind, innovative, trailblazer
- Vision-setting; goal-oriented; supportive
- Transparent, inclusive, strategic
- Brave, authentic, responsible
- Vision, courage and determination, ability to inspire and motivate others
- Collaboration, understanding, trust
- Culture bearer, sense maker, vision
- Listener, follower, decisive
- Facilitator, collaborator, guide

- One who encourages, supports, uplifts, educates, directs with humility and kindness and strength
- Courageous, supportive, accountable
- Accountability; vision; supportive
- Responsible, accountable, purposeful
- Responsible, respectful, reliable
- Advocate, courage, guide
- Responsibility over others
- Listen, weave, assess
- Development, mentorship (for self and others), and integrity
- Visionary, understanding, disciplined
- Motivator of people to get things done in a way that is aligned with shared goals and values. Three words: coach, strong, human
- Steward
- Inspirational, strategic, values-driven
- Facilitator, effective, compassionate
- A leader is someone who opens new paths for others
- Responsibility, compassion/care, vision
- Courageous, sincere, strategist
- Serve, support growth

How would you define power?

Primary themes:

Power as agency: Ability to influence, make decisions, impact change, inspire, sway, move an agenda, produce desired results, affect change, influence dollars and systems, have a voice, turn obstacles into opportunities, and self-knowledge.

Power with others: Collective power, creating space for others, care and consideration for equity, facilitating, empowering, accountability, and relationships.

Power as negative: White, male, and hierarchical; positions and titles; making decisions on behalf of rather than with; top-down culture; lack of connection between capacity to create positive change and power; controlling; withheld from some groups of people.

Dimensions/types of power: Collective power; formal or informal; connected to resources; internal and external; inner power; positional power; internalized power; having different levels of power in different contexts.

In what ways, if any, do you believe your leadership differs from traditional leadership?

Primary themes:

Relational and collaborative: collaboration and advancement of the collective; more relational than transactional; collaborative leader; not having power over; nurturing the careers of people; trust; deep relationship-building; mentoring; ensuring others have the space they need; build resilient teams; shared power; facilitative; others have space; build relationships with my team; more collaborative and intentionally inclusive; tuned into feelings and perspectives; foster a collective; hold space in a group; people-centered; not singular or based on individual power; mindful of how much space I take up as a leader.

Inclusive: dislike for top-down leadership; valuing difference and inclusion; open-minded; listening; center DEI principles; equity and respect are central to every decision; center experiences and needs of those at the margins; being more inclusive; able to see different points of view; focused on the collective.

Values-based: modeling values; reinforce our values; lead by example; deeply rooted and non-negotiable beliefs; humility; empathetic; honest; compassionate.

Culture-focus: important culture-setting role; embrace and amplify culture as integral to freedom and liberation; different time expectations.

Leadership qualities: see many steps ahead; emergent; innovative; take more risks; outside what is expected; creative; transparent; more experimentation and risk-taking; showing vulnerability but not too much.

What have been the top two or three obstacles you've faced as a woman of color leader?

Primary themes:

Lack of support: lack of support from my people; lack of respect from outside; feeling isolated and alone; lack of mentors who share my experience; not having a mentor in my life; lack of guidance and coaching; white women question my right to be in positions of power and at times even organize campaigns to discredit me; white men in particular talk down to me and question my expertise.

Lack of access: lack of opportunities for advancement; trying to break the barrier and be offered a chance to demonstrate my gifts; glass ceiling; deliberate exclusion from opportunities.

Perceptions: people don't assume I am a leader; men who are afraid of women who know more than they do; perceived as being nice or compliant; referred to as 'non-threatening'; seen as too emotional, unbalanced, unstable; deemed unsophisticated; cultural outsider; invisible, overlooked, unimportant; assumptions of ineptitude; being underestimated and undervalued;

Internal obstacles: I am my biggest critic; moments of self-doubt and over-deference to others; imposter syndrome; lack of confidence to negotiate a higher salary.

What does/would a workplace culture that is nurturing to your leadership look and feel like?

Primary themes:

Collaborative: sharing ideas and strategies, even when we may differ on views and approaches; working diligently and not dumping their job responsibilities on others; effective teamwork (communication, coordination, facilitation, taking the initiative); shared voice; a celebration of different approaches, ways of seeing; people toward the larger good; transparent with one another and not afraid to share their skills; understands how people can have different abilities and bring their abilities together to achieve their goals; truly collaborative and supportive of growth and learning; boundaries are collaboratively set and respected; colleagues don't undermine each other; power is not hoarded or wielded against, or in support of anyone, and boundaries are collaboratively set and respected.

Supportive, inclusive, and open: open to and supportive of risk-taking; invested in my development as a leader; not having to work twice as hard every day to be valued like in other organizations; not having to expend energy on making sure my manager isn't threatened by me and my abilities; not having to expend energy on making others comfortable or people-pleasing; open to different leadership styles; supportive colleagues and board members; promotes my growth and development; more emphasis on inclusion; workplace culture that is nurturing and inclusive; realistic goals that help set boundaries; agreed upon expectations; access to affinity groups/spaces; recognition and appreciation; resources and restoration; workplace culture where people can bring their whole self to work; a staff that understands and appreciates the complexity and challenges of leadership; a place where I can thrive, make decisions, be creative, and challenge the bosses; celebration of different approaches, ways of seeing; where people don't look at me as a diverse hire, but as a qualified professional; allows room for mistakes and risk-taking.

Trusting and transparent: trust; trusting my skills, lived experience, and approach; multiple identities at the decision-making table, valuing multiple ways of being; challenge of whiteness; safe to express my concerns and experiences without fear; transparency; everyone is transparent with one another and not afraid to share their skills; built on true trust, honesty, and authenticity; open and honest.

Caring: allows staff to be human; community values allow differences in style but discourage/constrain intolerance and toxic behaviors that undercut others' learning and motivation to meet the mission; supported in showing up as my whole strong, powerful, human, imperfect self; peaceful place to be; a culture where I'm not always playing defensive; interest in my well-being; communication and self-care are priorities and not afterthoughts; culture of rest, where we are not expected to be constantly available, or acting from a place of urgency.

Notes

Preface

1 bell hooks, *Yearning: Race, Gender, and Cultural Politics* (United Kingdom: Taylor & Francis, 2014), 229.

2 Ruchika Tulshyan, *Inclusion on Purpose: An Intersectional Approach to Creating a Culture of Belonging at Work* (United States: MIT Press, 2022), 57.

3 Cyndi Suarez, *The Power Manual: How to Master Complex Power Dynamics* (Canada: New Society Publishers, 2018).

4 Robin DiAngelo, "No, I Won't Stop Saying 'White Supremacy,'" *YES!* magazine, June 30, 2017, www.yesmagazine.org/democracy/2017/06/30/no-i -wont-stop-saying-white-supremacy.

5 Catherine Nash, "Patriarchy: An Overview," Science Direct, 2020, www .sciencedirect.com/topics/social-sciences/patriarchy.

6 Cedric J. Robinson, *Cedric J. Robinson: On Racial Capitalism, Black Internationalism, and Cultures of Resistance*, ed. H. L. T. Quan (Pluto Press, 2019), https://doi.org/10.2307/j.ctvr0qs8p.

Introduction

1 Donna Hicks, "What Is the Real Meaning of Dignity?" *Psychology Today*, April 10, 2013, www.psychologytoday.com/us/blog/dignity/201304/what -is-the-real-meaning-dignity-0.

2 Aysa Gray, "The Bias of 'Professionalism' Standards," *Stanford Social Innovation Review*, June 4, 2019, https://ssir.org/articles/entry/the_bias _of_professionalism_standards.

3 Gabriela Alcalde, "The Practice of Community as Murmuration," Medium, September 29, 2022, https://medium.com/@alcaldegabriela3/the-practice -of-community-as-murmuration-7f818f634960.

4 adrienne maree brown, *We Will Not Cancel Us: And Other Dreams of Transformative Justice* (United States: AK Press, 2020).

5 Kristin A. Neff, *Fierce Self-Compassion: How Women Can Harness Kindness to Speak Up, Claim Their Power, and Thrive* (United States: Penguin, 2021), 72.

6 "Racial Equity Principles," White Supremacy Culture, n.d., www.white
supremacyculture.info/racial-equity-principles.html.

7 Hila Mehr, "Cultivating Empathy and Internal Awareness for Social
Change," July 30, 2014, https://hilamehr.com/2014/07/30/cultivating
-empathy-and-internal-awareness-for-social-change.

Section 1. Claiming Space by Telling Our Stories

1 Elizabeth Leiba, *I'm Not Yelling: A Black Woman's Guide to Navigating the
Workplace* (United States: Mango Media, n.d.), 162.

Chapter 1. Understanding the Difference between Safety and Comfort

1 "How Leaders Can Build Psychological Safety at Work," Center for
Creative Leadership, April 10, 2024, www.ccl.org/articles/leading
-effectively-articles/what-is-psychological-safety-at-work.

2 Gail Christopher and Deepa Iyer, "Honoring and Supporting Women of
Color Leaders," *Stanford Social Innovation Review,* April 4, 2023, https://
doi.org/10.48558/DQ20-7G23.

Chapter 2. Talking about Racism Is Hard

1 Andrea J. Rogers and Tiloma Jayasinghe, "The Hidden Cost of DEI Work—
and What to Do about It," *Nonprofit Quarterly*, August 5, 2021, https://
nonprofitquarterly.org/the-hidden-cost-of-dei-work-and-what-to-do
-about-it.

Chapter 3. Checking the Boxes

1 Ruchika Tulshyan and Jodi-Ann Burey, "Stop Telling Women They Have
Imposter Syndrome," *Harvard Business Review*, February 11, 2021, https://
hbr.org/2021/02/stop-telling-women-they-have-imposter-syndrome.

2 "Racial Capitalism," Stone Inequality Initiative, Brown University, n.d.,
accessed February 25, 2024, https://watson.brown.edu/stoneinequality
/bibliography/2022/racial-capitalism.

Chapter 4. White People Tell Me Who I Am

1 john a. powell and Stephen Menendian, "The Problem of Othering:
Towards Inclusiveness and Belonging," Othering & Belonging Institute,
June 29, 2017, www.otheringandbelonging.org/the-problem-of-othering.

Chapter 5. (Invisible) Structural Barriers to Leadership and Leadership Resources

1 Monique Judge, "Professionalism Is a Racist Construct," *Dame* magazine, May 18, 2022, www.damemagazine.com/2022/05/18/professionalism -is-a-racist-construct.

2 Mark Horoszowski, "How to Build a Great Relationship with a Mentor," *Harvard Business Review*, January 21, 2020, https://hbr.org/2020/01/how -to-build-a-great-relationship-with-a-mentor.

3 "Race to Lead: Women of Color in the Nonprofit Sector," Building Movement Project, n.d., accessed February 25, 2024, https://buildingmovement .org/reports/race-to-lead-women-of-color-in-the-nonprofit-sector.

Chapter 6. Don't Tell Me about It

1 Jenae Holloway, "White People: Your Comfort Is Not Our Problem," *Vogue*, June 11, 2020, www.vogue.com/article/white-people-your-comfort-is-not -my-problem-black-lives-matter.

2 Holloway, "Your Comfort Is Not Our Problem."

3 Natalie Walrond, "Decolonize Your Board," *Stanford Social Innovation Review*, Summer 2021, https://ssir.org/pdf/Summer-2021-Feature -Walrond-Decolonize-Board.pdf.

4 Walrond, "Decolonize Your Board."

5 Aracely Muñoz, "Nonprofit Boards Efforts to Diversify," *Nonprofit Quarterly*, April 17, 2023, https://nonprofitquarterly.org/nonprofit-boards -efforts-to-diversify.

6 Muñoz, "Nonprofit Boards Efforts to Diversify."

7 Muñoz, "Nonprofit Boards Efforts to Diversify."

8 Muñoz, "Nonprofit Boards Efforts to Diversify."

9 Peter Dobkin Hall, *A History of Nonprofit Boards in the United States*, Board-Source, 2003, www.ncfp.org/wp-content/uploads/2018/09/A-History -of-Nonprofit-Boards-in-the-United-States-BoardSource-2003-a-history -of-nonprofit-boards-in-the-united-states.pdf, p. 4.

10 Judith L. Millesen, "Who 'Owns' Your Nonprofit?" *Nonprofit Quarterly*, August 13, 2019, https://nonprofitquarterly.org/who-owns-your-nonprofit.

11 Vu, "Why Do So Many Nice People Become Assholes When They Join a Board?" Nonprofit AF, May 22, 2023, https://nonprofitaf.com/2023/05 /why-do-so-many-nice-people-become-assholes-when-they-join-a-board.

12 Brené Brown, "Brené and Barrett on Why Every Leader Needs to Worry about Toxic Culture," *Dare to Lead* (podcast), April 4, 2022, https://brenebrown .com/podcast/why-every-leader-needs-to-worry-about-toxic-culture.

Chapter 7. White Supremacy Is the Air We All Breathe

1 Suarez, *Power Manual*, 17.
2 Edgar Villanueva, *Decolonizing Wealth: Indigenous Wisdom to Heal Divides and Restore Balance* (United States: Berrett-Koehler, 2018).
3 Jennifer Magley, "How Toxic Work Culture Breeds Unnecessary Competition between Black Employees," *Forbes*, February 14, 2023, www.forbes .com/sites/jennifermagley/2023/02/14/how-toxic-work-culture-breeds -unnecessary-competition-between-black-employees.
4 M. Cristina Alcalde and Mangala Subramaniam, "Gendering and Racializing Contemporary Leadership in Higher Education," in *Dismantling Institutional Whiteness: Emerging Forms of Leadership in Higher Education*, ed. M. Cristina Alcalde and Mangala Subramaniam (United States: Purdue University Press, 2022), 10.
5 Allaija Briann Williams, "The Implications of Colorism on Black Women from the Early 20th Century to the Present," (Honors thesis, University of Southern Mississippi, May 2022), https://aquila.usm.edu/honors_theses /839; Luis Noe-Bustamante, Ana Gonzalez-Barrera, Khadijah Edwards, Lauren Mora, and Mark Hugo Lopez, "Latinos and Colorism: Majority of Latinos Say Skin Color Impacts Opportunity in America and Shapes Daily Life," Pew Research Center, November 4, 2021, www.pewresearch.org /hispanic/2021/11/04/majority-of-latinos-say-skin-color-impacts -opportunity-in-america-and-shapes-daily-life.
6 Ruchika T. Malhotra, "How Colorism Affects Women at Work," *Harvard Business Review*, April 7, 2023, https://hbr.org/2023/04/how-colorism -affects-women-at-work.
7 Janice Gassam Asare, "Dr. Sarah L. Webb Explores the Pervasiveness of Colorism within Society," *Forbes*, February 1, 2022, www.forbes.com/sites /janicegassam/2022/01/28/dr-sarah-l-webb-explores-the-pervasiveness -of-colorism-within-society.
8 Suarez, *Power Manual*, 61.

Chapter 8. Divide and Conquer

1 Courtland Milloy, "How American Oligarchs Created the Concept of Race to Divide and Conquer the Poor," *Washington Post*, April 19, 2016,

www.washingtonpost.com/local/how-wealthy-americans-divided-and
-conquered-the-poor-to-create-the-concept-of-race/2016/04/19/2cab6e38
-0643-11e6-b283-e79d81c63c1b_story.html.

2 Judge, "Professionalism Is a Racist Construct."

3 David J. Smith, "Free Yourself From the Golden Handcuffs for a More
Purposeful Career," *Forbes*, November 4, 2020, www.forbes.com/sites
/forbescoachescouncil/2020/11/04/free-yourself-from-the-golden
-handcuffs-for-a-more-purposeful-career.

4 David Burkus, "Why a Company Is Not a Family—and How Companies
Can Bond with Their Employees Instead," TED.com, January 19, 2022,
https://ideas.ted.com/why-a-company-is-not-a-family-and-how
-companies-can-bond-with-their-employees-instead.

Chapter 9. Having the Last Word

1 Deepa Purushothaman, "Stop Telling Young Women of Color to Accept a
Broken System," *Harvard Business Review*, June 22, 2022, https://hbr.org
/2022/06/stop-telling-young-women-of-color-to-accept-a-broken-system.

2 Lawrence Glickman, "How White Backlash Controls American Progress,"
Atlantic, May 21, 2020, www.theatlantic.com/ideas/archive/2020/05/white
-backlash-nothing-new/611914.

Chapter 10. When White Women Do White Supremacy's Dirty Work

1 Heather Laine Talley, "White Women Doing White Supremacy in
Nonprofit Culture," Equity in the Center, September 25, 2019, https://
equityinthecenter.org/white-women-doing-white-supremacy-in
-nonprofit-culture.

2 Jane Coaston, "The Intersectionality Wars," Vox, May 28, 2019, www.vox
.com/the-highlight/2019/5/20/18542843/intersectionality-conservatism
-law-race-gender-discrimination.

3 UN PRPD and UN Women, *Intersectionality Resource Guide and Toolkit: An
Intersectional Approach to Leave No One Behind*, n.d., https://www.unwomen
.org/sites/default/files/2022-01/Intersectionality-resource-guide-and-toolkit
-en.pdf.

Chapter 11. You Just Sound So Confident and Competent

1 Erika Gutierrez, Janét Hund, Shaheen Johnson, Carlos Ramos, Lisette
Rodriguez, and Joy Tsuhako, "Whiteness: White Privilege, White Supremacy, and White Fragility," LibreTexts Social Sciences, March 5, 2020,

https://socialsci.libretexts.org/Courses/Long_Beach_City_College
/Race_and_Ethnic_Relations_in_the_U.S.%3A_An_Intersectional
_Approach/06%3A_Euro_Americans_and_Whiteness/6.03%3A
_Whiteness-__White_Privilege_White_Supremacy_and_White_Fragility.

2 Kira Page, "The 'Problem' Woman of Colour in NonProfit Organizations,"
   COCo, March 8, 2018, https://coco-net.org/problem-woman-colour
   -nonprofit-organizations.

3 Kecia M. Thomas, Juanita Johnson-Bailey, Rosemary E. Phelps, Ny Mia
   Tran, and Lindsay Johnson, "Women of Color at Midcareer: Going from
   Pet to Threat," in *The Psychological Health of Women of Color: Intersections,
   Challenges, and Opportunities*, ed. Lillian Comas-Díaz and Beverly Greene,
   275–86 (United States: Guilford Press, 2013).

4 Erika Stallings, "When Black Women Go from Office Pet to Office Threat,"
   Medium, January 16, 2020, https://zora.medium.com/when-black-women
   -go-from-office-pet-to-office-threat-83bde710332e.

5 Vu, "Outsider Efficacy Bias: What It Is and How It Affects Our Work," Nonprofit AF, November 15, 2021, https://nonprofitaf.com/2021/11/outsider
   -efficacy-bias-what-it-is-and-how-it-affects-our-work/.

6 Christopher and Iyer, "Honoring and Supporting Women of Color Leaders."

7 Sida Ly-Xiong, "Leading Together for Systems Change," *Stanford Social
   Innovation Review*, March 22, 2023, https://ssir.org/articles/entry
   /leading_together_for_systems_change.

Chapter 12. Complicit Silence

1 Tsedale M. Melaku, Angie Beeman, David G. Smith, and W. Brad Johnson,
   "Be a Better Ally," *Harvard Business Review*, November 1, 2020, https://
   hbr.org/2020/11/be-a-better-ally.

Chapter 14. The Added Burden and Toll of Unpaid and Unseen Emotional Labor

1 Dnika J. Travis and Jennifer Thorpe-Moscon, "Day-to-Day Experiences of
   Emotional Tax among Women and Men of Color in the Workplace," Catalyst, www.catalyst.org/wp-content/uploads/2019/02/emotionaltax.pdf.

2 Travis and Thorpe-Moscon, "Day-to-Day Experiences of Emotional Tax."

3 Enlightened-Solutions, "Emotional Labor of Women of Color in the Workplace," Medium, August 10, 2021, https://medium.com/workenlightened
   /emotional-labor-of-women-of-color-in-the-workplace-5902836cfa34.

4 Jean Chen Ho, "Bling Empire and the Energizing Potential of Asian-American
   Mediocrity," *Harper's Bazaar*, February 17, 2021, www.harpersbazaar.com
   /culture/film-tv/a35522226/bling-empire-and-the-energizing-potential
   -of-asian-american-mediocrity.

5 Cristina Alcalde, "The Burnout Is Real—but This Is Nothing New for Women of Color," *Ms.* magazine, October 28, 2021, https://msmagazine.com/2021/10/28/women-workers-covid-burnout.

6 Travis and Thorpe-Moscon, "Day-to-Day Experiences of Emotional Tax."

7 Hanieh Khosroshahi, "The Concrete Ceiling," *Stanford Social Innovation Review*, May 10, 2021, https://ssir.org/articles/entry/the_concrete_ceiling.

Section 4. The System Will Not Be Complicit in Its Own Demise

1 Vu, "No, Social Enterprise and Earned Revenues Will Not Solve Nonprofits' Funding Problems," Nonprofit AF, April 4, 2023, https://nonprofitaf.com/2023/04/no-social-enterprise-and-earned-revenues-will-not-solve-nonprofits-funding-problems.

2 "Building Prisms of the People within the Nonprofit Industrial Complex," HistPhil, March 23, 2022, https://histphil.org/2022/03/23/building-prisms-of-the-people-within-the-nonprofit-industrial-complex.

3 "Building Prisms of the People," HistPhil.

4 Hildy Gottlieb, "How Nonprofits Can Truly Advance Change," *Nonprofit Quarterly*, January 25, 2022, https://nonprofitquarterly.org/how-nonprofits-can-truly-advance-change.

Chapter 15. Understanding and Recreating the Container

1 "CF Insights Survey Results," Council on Foundations, August 14, 2023, https://cof.org/cfinsights/results.

2 Patricia Arboleda, "The Real Reason Latinas Are Exiting the Job Market," *Hispanic Executive*, March 29, 2022. https://hispanicexecutive.com/the-real-reason-latinas-are-exiting-the-job-market.

3 "Grantmaker Salary and Benefits Report," Council on Foundations, September 14, 2022, https://cof.org/grantmaker-salary-benefits.

4 Native Americans in Philanthropy and Candid, *Investing in Native Communities: Philanthropic Funding for Native American Communities and Causes*, 2019, https://nativephilanthropy.candid.org; Hilda Vega, "Funding for Latinx Populations in the U.S," Hispanics in Philanthropy, n.d., accessed March 3, 2024, https://hipfunds.org/updated-latinxfunders-dashboard; Ben Barge, Brandi Collins-Calhoun, Elbert Garcia, Jeanné Lewis, Janay Richmond, Ryan Schlegel, Spencer Ozer, and Stephanie Peng, "Black Funding Denied: Community Foundation Support for Black Communities," National Committee for Responsive Philanthropy, August 26, 2020, https://ncrp.org/2020/08/black-funding-denied.

5 *Nonprofit Compensation Report*, Candid, 2020, https://www.guidestar.org/nonprofit-compensation-report/.

6 Jim Rendon, "Why Women Don't Get Ahead at Nonprofits," *Chronicle of Philanthropy*, January 12, 2021, www.philanthropy.com/article/why-women-dont-get-ahead.

7 *Making (or Taking) Space: Initial Themes on Nonprofit Transitions from White to BIPOC Leaders*, Building Movement Project, September 2021, https://static1.squarespace.com/static/58c4168af5e23157c0a605ac/t/6165966613b6bd559d024a91/1634047590328/Making+Or+Taking+Space.pdf; *Trading Glass Ceilings for Glass Cliffs: A Race to Lead Report on Nonprofit Executives of Color*, Building Movement Project, 2022, https://buildingmovement.org/reports/trading-glass-ceilings-for-glass-cliffs-a-race-to-lead-report-on-nonprofit-executives-of-color.

8 William H. Frey, "Even as Metropolitan Areas Diversify, White Americans Still Live in Mostly White Neighborhoods," Brookings, March 23, 2020, www.brookings.edu/articles/even-as-metropolitan-areas-diversify-white-americans-still-live-in-mostly-white-neighborhoods.

9 Anna Sale and Shereen Marisol Meraji, "Code Switch: Cross-Racial Relationships," NPR, January 27, 2020, www.npr.org/2020/01/27/799925293/code-switch-cross-racial-relationships.

10 Emily Field, Alexis Krivkovich, Sandra Kügele, Nicole Robinson, and Lareina Yee, *Women in the Workplace 2023*, McKinsey & Company, October 5, 2023, www.mckinsey.com/featured-insights/diversity-and-inclusion/women-in-the-workplace.

11 Field et al., *Women in the Workplace 2023*.

12 *State of Inequity*, Hue, n.d., accessed July 18, 2024, www.wearehue.org/stateofinequity; Kim Parker and Juliana Menasce Horowitz, "Majority of Workers Who Quit a Job in 2021 Cite Low Pay, No Opportunities for Advancement, Feeling Disrespected," Pew Research Center, March 9, 2022, www.pewresearch.org/fact-tank/2022/03/09/majority-of-workers-who-quit-a-job-in-2021-cite-low-pay-no-opportunities-for-advancement-feeling-disrespected.

13 *State of Inequity*, Hue.

14 Erynn Beaton and Megan LePere-Schloop, "3 in 4 Fundraisers Have Experienced Sexual Harassment on the Job—Often Because of Inappropriate Behavior from Donors," The Conversation, May 26, 2022, https://theconversation.com/3-in-4-fundraisers-have-experienced-sexual-harassment-on-the-job-often-because-of-inappropriate-behavior-from-donors-183332.

15 Ana Sandoiu, "'Weathering': What Are the Health Effects of Stress and Discrimination," Medical News Today, February 26, 2021, www.medicalnewstoday.com/articles/weathering-what-are-the-health-effects-of-stress-and-discrimination.

16 Bob Weinhold, "Epigenetics: The Science of Change," *Environmental Health Perspectives* 114, no. 3 (March 1, 2006), https://doi.org/10.1289 /ehp.114-a160; Sue Coyle, "Intergenerational Trauma—Legacies of Loss," *Social Work Today* 14, no. 3 (2014), www.socialworktoday.com/archive /051214p18.shtml.

17 "NIH-Funded Study Highlights Stark Racial Disparities in Maternal Deaths," National Institutes of Health, August 12, 2021, www.nih.gov/news-events /news-releases/nih-funded-study-highlights-stark-racial-disparities -maternal-deaths.

18 Aditya Aladangady and Akila Forde, "Wealth Inequality and the Racial Wealth Gap," FEDS Notes, Board of Governors of the Federal Reserve System, October 22, 2021, www.federalreserve.gov/econres/notes/feds -notes/wealth-inequality-and-the-racial-wealth-gap-20211022.htm.

19 "Race and Ethnicity," Prison Policy Initiative, updated August 28, 2024, www.prisonpolicy.org/research/race_and_ethnicity.

20 "Reducing the Racial Homeownership Gap," Urban Institute, May 31, 2019, www.urban.org/policy-centers/housing-finance-policy-center/projects /reducing-racial-homeownership-gap.

21 GBD 2019 Police Violence US Subnational Collaborators, "Fatal Police Violence by Race and State in the USA, 1980–2019: A Network Meta-Regression," *Lancet* 398, no. 10307 (October 2, 2021): 1239–55, https:// doi.org/10.1016/S0140-6736(21)01609-3.

22 Derecka Purnell, "The 'Missing White Woman Syndrome' Still Plagues America," *Guardian*, September 29, 2021, www.theguardian.com /commentisfree/2021/sep/29/the-missing-white-woman-syndrome-still -plagues-america.

23 Elise Gould and Valerie Wilson, "Black Workers Face Two of the Most Lethal Preexisting Conditions for Coronavirus—Racism and Economic Inequality," Economic Policy Institute, June 1, 2020, www.epi.org/publication/black -workers-covid/#wage-gaps.

24 Elizabeth Castillo, "Walking the Talk: Reclaiming Dignity through Human-istic Management," *Nonprofit Quarterly*, June 14, 2022, https://nonprofit quarterly.org/walking-the-talk-reclaiming-dignity-through-humanistic -management.

Chapter 16. Containers of Culture

1 Yonason Goldson, "This Is the Secret to Healing a Toxic Culture," *Fast Company*, April 16, 2023, www.fastcompany.com/90881819/this-is-the-secret-to -healing-a-toxic-culture.

2 Christopher and Iyer, "Honoring and Supporting Women of Color Leaders."

Chapter 17. Inspecting the Scaffolding

1   Design Studio for Social Intervention, "Ideas Arrangements Effects: Systems Design and Social Justice," *Nonprofit Quarterly*, July 13, 2020, https://nonprofitquarterly.org/ideas-arrangements-effects-systems-design-and-social-justice.
2   Design Studio for Social Intervention, "Ideas Arrangements Effects."
3   Melissa Gregg, "The Productivity Obsession," *Atlantic*, November 13, 2015, www.theatlantic.com/business/archive/2015/11/be-more-productive/415821.
4   Dismantling Racism Works, *White Supremacy Culture in Organizations*, adapted by the Centre for Community Organizations, n.d., accessed July 18, 2024, https://coco-net.org/wp-content/uploads/2019/11/Coco-WhiteSup Culture-ENG4.pdf.
5   Coaston, "Intersectionality Wars."
6   Lily Zheng, *DEI Deconstructed: Your No-Nonsense Guide to Doing the Work and Doing It Right* (United States: Berrett-Koehler, 2022).
7   Jeanne Bell, Dominique Samari, and Steve Zimmerman, "Process and Practice: Linking Organizational Strategy and Race Equity Work," *Nonprofit Quarterly*, March 1, 2022, https://nonprofitquarterly.org/process-and-practice-linking-organizational-strategy-and-race-equity-work.
8   Caitlin C. Rosenthal, "How Slavery Inspired Modern Business Management," *Boston Review*, August 20, 2018, www.bostonreview.net/articles/caitlin-c-rosenthal-accounting-slavery-excerpt.
9   Kim-Monique Johnson, "How to Be an Antiracist Supervisor: Start with Changing What You Call Yourself," *Nonprofit Quarterly*, April 15, 2021, https://nonprofitquarterly.org/how-to-be-an-antiracist-supervisor-start-with-changing-what-you-call-yourself.
10 Frederic Laloux, *Reinventing Organizations: A Guide to Creating Organizations Inspired by the Next Stage of Human Consciousness* (Belgium: Nelson Parker, 2014).
11 "Developmental Perspective on Organizations," Reinventing Organizations Wiki," n.d., accessed June 7, 2024, https://reinventingorganizationswiki.com/en/theory/developmental-perspective-on-organizations.
12 "Learning out Loud: Lessons from Our Community," Trust-Based Philanthropy Project, n.d., accessed February 25, 2024, www.trustbasedphilanthropy.org/blog-1/2/25/22-lessons-from-our-community.
13 Building Movement Project and BoardSource, *Avoiding the Glass Cliff: Advice to Boards on Preparing for and Supporting a New Leader of Color*, n.d., accessed February 25, 2024, https://boardsource.org/wp-content/uploads/2022/05/Avoiding-Glass-Cliff.pdf.

Chapter 18. Leading for Survival, Leading for Liberation

1 Laura Escobar-Ratliff, "Self-Care A-Z: Celebrating Hispanic-Latinx Heritage Month—Promoting Expansive Self-Care," *New Social Worker*, October 2022, www.socialworker.com/feature-articles/self-care/celebrating-hispanic -latinx-heritage-month-expansive-self-care.

2 Faima Bakar, "There's No Such Thing as a Dream Job, No One Aspires to Do Labour," HuffPost UK, May 16, 2022, www.huffingtonpost.co.uk/entry /theres-no-such-thing-as-a-dream-job_uk_627ce63ee4b06ce0a1b2afa8.

3 Tish Harrison Warren, "How To Fight Back Against the Inhumanity of Modern Work," *New York Times*, October 16, 2022, www.nytimes.com /2022/10/16/opinion/work-rest-sabbath.html.

4 Christopher and Iyer, "Honoring and Supporting Women of Color Leaders."

5 Anne Helen Petersen, "The Wages of Overwork," Culture Study, April 19, 2023, https://annehelen.substack.com/p/the-wages-of-overwork.

6 Petersen, "Wages of Overwork."

7 Jonnelle Marte and Lucia Mutikani, "Share of U.S. Workers Holding Multiple Jobs Is Rising, New Census Report Shows," Reuters, February 2021, https://www.reuters.com/article/idUSKBN2AH2PH.

8 Mistinguette Smith, "Racial Justice Backlash, Burnout, and POC Leaders," July 14, 2021, www.msmithconsulting.net/blog/2021/7/14/racial-justice -backlash-burnout-and-poc-leaders.

9 Rachel Hislop, "'It's Not Just Burnout:' How Grind Culture Fails Women," Pocket, n.d., accessed February 25, 2024, https://getpocket.com/collections /its-not-just-burnout-how-grind-culture-failed-women.

10 U.S. Bureau of Labor Statistics, "Labor Force Characteristics by Race and Ethnicity, 2022," November 2023. www.bls.gov/opub/reports/race-and -ethnicity/2022/home.htm.

11 Dany Sigwalt, "How to Prevent Burnout among Black Movement Leaders," *YES!* magazine, February 23, 2022, www.yesmagazine.org/opinion/2022 /02/23/stop-burnout-among-black-movement-leaders.

12 R. van den Bosch, T. W. Taris, W. B. Schaufeli, M. C. W. Peeters, and G. Reijseger, "Authenticity at Work: A Matter of Fit?" *Journal of Psychology: Interdisciplinary and Applied* 153, no. 2 (2019): 247–66, https://doi.org /10.1080/00223980.2018.1516185.

13 Alcalde and Subramaniam, *Dismantling Institutional Whiteness*, 6.

14 Cyndi Suarez, "What Does It Look Like to Support Women of Color to Lead?" *Nonprofit Quarterly*, January 4, 2021, https://nonprofitquarterly .org/what-does-it-look-like-to-support-women-of-color-to-lead.

Section 5. Leading Outside the Lines

1 Tony Gambill, "Why Self-Leadership Is the Most Important Leadership," *Forbes*, April 8, 2021, www.forbes.com/sites/tonygambill/2021/04/08/why-self-leadership-is-the-most-important-leadership.

2 Idalia Fernandez and Lori Bartczak, "Leadership Development Programs Need an Upgrade: Five Ways to Advance Racial Equity," Race to Lead, March 31, 2022, https://racetolead.org/leadership-development-programs-need-an-upgrade-five-ways-to-advance-racial-equity.

3 Deborah Bae and Kiernan Doherty, "The Need for More Inclusive Leadership Narratives," *Stanford Social Innovation Review*, February 22, 2023, https://ssir.org/articles/entry/the_need_for_more_inclusive_leadership_narratives.

4 Hanieh Khosroshahi, "The Concrete Ceiling," *Stanford Social Innovation Review*, May 10, 2021, https://ssir.org/articles/entry/the_concrete_ceiling.

5 Sida Ly-Xiong, "Leading Together for Systems Change," *Stanford Social Innovation Review*, March 22, 2023, https://ssir.org/articles/entry/leading_together_for_systems_change.

6 Don Waisanen, *Leadership Standpoints: A Practical Framework for the Next Generation of Nonprofit Leaders* (United Kingdom: Cambridge University Press, 2021), 65, https://doi.org/10.1017/9781009000284.

7 Ly-Xiong, "Leading Together for Systems Change."

8 Darren Isom, Cora Daniels, and Britt Savage, "What Everyone Can Learn from Leaders of Color," *Stanford Social Innovation Review*, June 28, 2022, https://ssir.org/articles/entry/what_everyone_can_learn_from_leaders_of_color.

9 Isom, Daniels, and Savage, "What Everyone Can Learn."

Chapter 19. Dreaming of a New Way

1 Waisanen, *Leadership Standpoints*, 65.

2 Suarez, *Power Manual*, 11.

3 "Power," JASS, n.d., accessed July 18, 2024, https://justassociates.org/what-we-do/power.

4 "The CEO's Role in Organizational Transformation," The Systems Thinker, January 19, 2016, https://thesystemsthinker.com/the-ceos-role-in-organizational-transformation.

5 Brené Brown, *Dare to Lead: Brave Work. Tough Conversations. Whole Hearts* (United Kingdom: Random House, 2018).

6 Suarez, *Power Manual*, 38.

7 Jeanne Bell, "Why Staff Structure Matters (a Lot)," JustOrg Design, March 2023, www.justorgdesign.com/post/why-staff-structure-matters.

8 Yolanda Contreras, "What Working at a Flat Organization Has Taught Me about White Supremacy," CCF, July 8, 2021, https://communitycentric fundraising.org/2021/07/08/what-working-at-a-flat-organization-has -taught-me-about-white-supremacy.

9 Maurice Mitchell, "Building Resilient Organizations," The Forge, November 29, 2022, https://forgeorganizing.org/article/building-resilient -organizations.

Chapter 20. Dimensions of Care, Rest, and Healing

1 Bethany Johnson-Javois, "Rest Is Restorative, Healing." *St. Louis American*, May 7, 2023, www.stlamerican.com/your_health_matters/health_opinion/rest -is-restorative-healing/article_fbdd8c6c-ecc4-11ed-b51e-1702e8f2e55b.html.

2 Tricia Hersey, *Rest Is Resistance: A Manifesto* (United States: Little, Brown Spark, 2022), 12.

3 Yonason Gold, "This Is the Secret to Healing a Toxic Culture," *Fast Company*, April 16, 2023, https://www.fastcompany.com/90881819/this-is-the -secret-to-healing-a-toxic-culture.

4 Paul J. Zak, "The Neuroscience of Trust," *Harvard Business Review*, 2017, https://hbr.org/2017/01/the-neuroscience-of-trust.

5 Carolyn O'Hara, "Proven Ways to Earn Your Employees' Trust," *Harvard Business Review*, June 27, 2014, https://hbr.org/2014/06/proven-ways -to-earn-your-employees-trust.

6 Brown, *Dare to Lead*.

7 Teju Ravilochan, "The Blackfoot Wisdom That Inspired Maslow's Hierarchy," Resilience, June 18, 2021, www.resilience.org/stories/2021-06-18 /the-blackfoot-wisdom-that-inspired-maslows-hierarchy.

8 Ravilochan, "Blackfoot Wisdom."

9 Ravilochan, "Blackfoot Wisdom."

10 Loretta Pyles, *Healing Justice: Holistic Self-Care for Change Makers* (United States: Oxford University Press, 2018), xviii.

11 Angela Blackwell, "The Curb-Cut Effect," *Stanford Social Innovation Review*, Winter 2017, https://ssir.org/articles/entry/the_curb_cut_effect.

12 Blackwell, "Curb-Cut Effect."

13 Audre Lorde, *A Burst of Light and Other Essays* (United States: Dover, 2017).

14 Yashna Maya Padamsee, "Communities of Care, Organizations for Liberation," Naya Maya, June 19, 2011, https://nayamaya.wordpress.com/2011 /06/19/communities-of-care-organizations-for-liberation.

15 Anne Helen Petersen, "How Our System Revenges Rest," Culture Study, November 21, 2021, https://annehelen.substack.com/p/how-our-system-revenges-rest.

16 Mariame Kaba, *We Do This 'Til We Free Us: Abolitionist Organizing and Transforming Justice* (United States: Haymarket Books, 2021)

Chapter 21. Beyond Us and Now

1 Mitchell, "Building Resilient Organizations."

2 Oliver Balch, "Buen Vivir: The Social Philosophy Inspiring Movements in South America," *Guardian*, February 4, 2013, www.theguardian.com/sustainable-business/blog/buen-vivir-philosophy-south-america-eduardo-gudynas.

3 Borna Jalsenjak, "Principle of Solidarity," in *Encyclopedia of Sustainable Management* (Springer: December 2019), https://doi.org/10.1007/978-3-030-02006-4_114-1.

4 Daniela Blei, "Diversity, Hierarchy, and Teamwork," *Stanford Social Innovation Review*, Summer 2022, https://ssir.org/articles/entry/diversity_hierarchy_and_teamwork.

5 john a. powell, Stephen Menendian, and Wendy Ake, "Targeted Universalism," Othering & Belonging Institute, updated December 2022, https://belonging.berkeley.edu/targeted-universalism.

6 The Design Studio for Social Intervention, *Ideas Arrangements Effects: Systems Design and Social Justice* (United States: Autonomedia, 2020).

7 Design Studio for Social Intervention, "Ideas Arrangements Effects."

8 Reinventing Organizations, www.reinventingorganizations.com.

9 Ted Rau, "Sociocracy: Basic Concepts and Principles," Sociocracy for All, August 2, 2020, www.sociocracyforall.org/sociocracy.

10 Holacracy, www.holacracy.org.

11 Tina Opie and Beth A. Livingston, *Shared Sisterhood: How to Take Collective Action for Racial and Gender Equity at Work* (United States: Harvard Business Review Press, 2022).

12 Cyndi Suarez, "The Sensemaking Organization: Designing for Complexity," *Nonprofit Quarterly*, April 16, 2019, https://nonprofitquarterly.org/the-sensemaking-organization-designing-for-complexity.

13 Elizabeth Castillo, "Walking the Talk: Reclaiming Dignity through Humanistic Management," *Nonprofit Quarterly*, June 14, 2022, https://nonprofitquarterly.org/walking-the-talk-reclaiming-dignity-through-humanistic-management.

14 Tiloma Jayasinghe, "Don't Rebuild, Upbuild!—Reimagining Nonprofit Infrastructure," *Nonprofit Quarterly*, October 19, 2021, https://nonprofit quarterly.org/dont-rebuild-upbuild-reimaging-nonprofit-infrastructure.

15 "Freedom Dreams in Philanthropy Is a Distinct Opportunity to Listen to and Leverage Visionary Leaders' Voices to Transform Our Institutions toward Justice," n.d., accessed February 25, 2024, www.freedomdreams philanthropy.org.

16 Cyndi Suarez, "Experiments in Liberatory Leadership," *Nonprofit Quarterly*, June 7, 2022, https://nonprofitquarterly.org/experiments-in-liberatory -leadership/.

17 Steven J. Cooper, "Donald O. Hebb's Synapse and Learning Rule: A History and Commentary," *Neuroscience & Biobehavioral Reviews* 28, no. 8 (January 2005): 851–74, https://doi.org/10.1016/j.neubiorev.2004.09.009.

Index

Tchume, Trish, 181
teal organizations, 184
teams, pod structure, 188–191
termination of employment, 80–83
    COBRA (Consolidated Omnibus
        Budget Reconciliation Act),
        79, 81
    retaliation for speaking up, 103
    severance packages, 57–58, 63–64
"There's No Such Thing As a Dream
    Job, No One Aspires to Do Labour"
    (Bakar), 149
"This Is the Secret to Healing a Toxic
    Culture" (Goldson), 172
Thomas, Kecia M., 97
tokenizing women of color, 27–31
tone-policing women of color, 94–95
*Trading Glass Ceilings for Glass
    Cliffs* report (Building Movement
    Project), 129–130
transformational power, 165
trust, 56, 172–173, 186
    linking trust and safety, 172
    power, 173
    workplace culture that is nurturing
        to leadership, 198
trust-based philanthropy (TBP), 146
Trust-Based Philanthropy Project,
    146, 173, 186
truth, 3–4
truth-telling, 10–11
Tulshyan, Ruchika, 29, 65, 70
Turner, Tina, 179

U

U.S. Bureau of Labor Statistics
    for-profit businesses failure rate,
        122
    loss of women from the labor
        market between 2020 and
        2022, 152
unexamined board, 56–58
United Nations Women, 90
United States Census 2020 data, 60–61

*Unsafe. Unheard. Unvalued. A State of
    Inequity* report (Hue), 132
upbuilding, 185
"The Uses of the Blues" (Baldwin), 27

V

values, 175
    capitalist, 150
    four Cs, 163–165
    non-traditional leadership, 196
Villanueva, Edgar, 129

W

"The Wages of Overwork"
    (Petersen), 150
Waisanen, Don, 160, 165
"Walking the Talk: Reclaiming Dignity
    through Humanistic Management"
    (Castillo), 171
Walrond, Natalie A., 59–60
Warren, Tish Harrison, 149–150
We Do This 'Til We Free Us (Kaba),
    15, 135
We Will Not Cancel Us (brown), 11
"What Everyone Can Learn from
    Leaders of Color" (Isom, Daniels,
    and Savage), 160–161
"What Working at a Flat Organization
    Has Taught Me about White
    Supremacy" (Contreras), 168
"When Black Women Go from
    Office Pet to Office Threat"
    (Thomas), 97
white backlash, 82
white comfort, omnipotence of,
    103–104
white fragility, 93–100
white saviorism, 186
white supremacy
    assumptions and assertions about
        identities of people of color,
        33–38
    boards, 59–62
    decolonizing boards, 59–60

social context, 132–134
white fragility manifesting for
  women of color, 93–100
WOC in nonprofits, 129–132
WOC in philanthropy, 125–127
workplace models, 186–191
  pod structure, 188–191

Y

Yulia (fear of strong women of color),
  93–94

Z

Zheng, Lily, 141

About the Author

Born in Lima, Peru, Gabriela Alcalde is a creative, anti-supremacist leader with experience in the philanthropic, academic, governmental, nonprofit, and grassroots sectors. She writes and speaks locally, nationally, and internationally about shifting the philanthropic and nonprofit sectors, racial justice, and leadership experience of women of color. She earned a bachelor's degree in psychology from the University of Louisville, a master's in public health from Boston University, and a doctorate in global public health from the University of North Carolina, Chapel Hill. *What Your Comfort Costs Us* is her first book.

About North Atlantic Books

North Atlantic Books (NAB) is an independent, nonprofit publisher committed to a bold exploration of the relationships between mind, body, spirit, and nature. Founded in 1974, NAB aims to nurture a holistic view of the arts, sciences, humanities, and healing. To make a donation or to learn more about our books, authors, events, and newsletter, please visit www.northatlanticbooks.com.